Dear Bill,

Mort would have loved to have given this to you.

With love and appreciation,

Maria-Pia

October 2013.

POMUS & SHUMAN
HITMAKERS
TOGETHER & APART

by Graham Vickers

POMUS & SHUMAN
HITMAKERS
TOGETHER & APART

by Graham Vickers

OMNIBUS PRESS
London / New York / Paris / Sydney / Copenhagen / Berlin / Madrid / Tokyo

ISBN: 978.1.78038.307.1
Order No: OP54461

Exclusive Distributors
Music Sales Limited,
14/15 Berners Street,
London, W1T 3LJ.

Music Sales Corporation
180 Madison Avenue, 24th Floor,
New York,
NY 10016,
USA.

Macmillan Distribution Services,
56 Parkwest Drive
Derrimut, Vic 3030,
Australia.

Typeset by Phoenix Photosetting, Chatham, Kent
Printed in the EU

A catalogue record for this book is available from the British Library.

Visit Omnibus Press on the web at www.omnibuspress.com

Contents

Introduction

Every generation gets the popular music it needs. In the early 1950s, as the sophisticated song writing of Jerome Kern, Irving Berlin, Johnny Mercer, Lorenz Hart, the Gershwins and the rest was starting to give way to the boisterous sounds of emergent white rock'n'roll, it was clear that the new generation of record buyers craved very different kinds of songs. Even Frank Sinatra, who had thought himself unassailably hip and cool, suddenly began to look dated – a swinger in a toupee who, in his late 30s, saw his career as a vocalist in free-fall as the Eddie Fishers and then the rock'n'rollers took over. Sinatra complained bitterly and he was not alone in bemoaning what he saw as a decline in musical standards. Out were the witty words and music of Cole Porter, Sammy Cahn and Jule Styne, and in were raucous blues pastiches like 'Hound Dog' (written by Jerry Leiber and Mike Stoller), concussive beat songs like 'Tutti Frutti' (written by Little Richard), and Elvis Presley's historic cover version of Arthur Crudup's blues song 'That's Alright Mama'. Meanwhile a whole clutch of grittier R&B-flavoured songs emerged with themes of thinly euphemised sex and violence expressed in a vernacular that owed little to the urbane lyrics of Lorenz Hart or Ira Gershwin.

The old guard believed that rock'n'roll was sounding the death knell of good song writing. Where, traditionalists wanted to know, were the new Gershwins, Kerns and Berlins to be found now that the barbarians were at the gates? Pleasingly there was a literal answer to this rhetorical question: they were to be found in mid-town Manhattan in a clutch of largely anonymous premises whose high profile focus was located at 1619 Broadway and 49th Street. The office building that stood there had once looked like nothing so much as a monument to bad timing when it was completed in 1931 less than two years after the Stock Market Crash. Its developer, Abraham E. Lefcourt, had already been obliged to trim his early ambitions to make it a rival to the exuberant 77-storey Chrysler Building but by the time it was finished at its new modest height of just 11 storeys, it had become painfully obvious that the brokers and bankers Lefcourt had assumed would rent its office space were by now out of business.

The Depression was underway and the only business that was thriving at all was the music business. Thus the Lefcourt Building (soon to be renamed The Brill Building) started its commercial life as a home to music publishers. Some of these specialised in publishing the music of black composers, some of whose instrumentals the publishers equipped with words written by white lyricists to make the result palatable to prevailing mainstream tastes. For example, Brill Building tenant Lewis Music only published black musician Erskine Hawkins' instrumental 'Tuxedo Junction' after it had been given lyrics by Buddy Feyne (Bernard Feinstein). Lewis then published some of Erskine Hawkins' songs as well as some by black pianist Avery Parrish. These were 'race music', the euphemism for songs written by black artists. If a composer wrote an instrumental (and even sometimes if there were already lyrics), the publishers provided their own lyricists. Top selling songs on the (white) Hit Parade, such as 'Tuxedo Junction' and 'Jersey Bounce', were originally composed as instrumentals by black swing artists, but were not played by white bands on the radio until they had been published with suitable lyrics, often by white writers. For this reason, the Brill Building publishers had become a focus for the music industry in New York, but by the late 1950s they were feeling the winds of change in musical taste as newer publishers sprang up. By the start of the 1960s there were over 120 independent music businesses in the building and many more dotted around the immediate neighbourhood, notably at 1650 Broadway, a nameless building that for a time housed more new publishers trying their luck than staid The Brill Building at number 1619.

The names that would emerge from this new Tin Pan Alley were Neil Sedaka & Howard Greenfield; Carole King & Gerry Goffin; Phillip Spector; Neil Diamond; Ellie Greenwich & Jeff Barry; Cynthia Weil & Barry Mann; and Jerome Felder & Mortimer Shuman.

Jerome Felder was better known by his self-anointed stage name Doc Pomus, and Shuman's first name was usually shortened to 'Mort' or 'Mortie'. Their imprimatur, however, as it traditionally appeared in parentheses on the record label beneath the song title was '[Pomus-Shuman]'.

For a generation of record buyers of a certain age that hybrid stamp all but guaranteed a superior pop song – or at least an interesting one. It came as a particularly welcome assurance when glimpsed on the 'B'-side of the single just purchased because it was the 'A'-side that was usually the known quantity – the reason for buying the record in the first place – so a Pomus-Shuman 'B'-side gave early indication that this was almost certainly money well spent. Sometimes it came as an extra blessing: those of us who bought 'Elvis Presley's '(Marie's The Name) His Latest Flame' (itself a Pomus-Shuman 'A'-side) were delighted to find it paired with another Pomus-Shuman composition, 'Little Sister'. 'Little Sister' soon promoted itself to the 'A'-side, became a hit, sounded like an instant classic and lived up to all its early promise with subsequent cover versions over the years by Ry Cooder, Dwight Yoakam and Robert Plant among others.

This book is an account of two overlapping lives that came together by chance to create pop music history in a few short years. By virtue of their age difference, Pomus and Shuman take centre stage both separately and together, their alliance barely spanning the decade between 1956 and 1966. What happened before and after that are this book's two other stories.

Finally it seems wise to give early notice that one ulterior motive in writing this book about two of my own adolescent heroes is to try to redress what I have long seen as a troubling imbalance. It has always been lyricist Doc Pomus – unquestionably a brave and talented man whose achievements against terrible physical odds deserve anyone's respect – who is celebrated as the star author of all those great songs. Mort has usually been presented as a colourful note in the margins of Doc's life, yet it was surely Mort whose achievements, in the end, were the greater. Perhaps that imbalance has something to do with American perceptions of American heroes. The triumph of the underdog is a heart-warming cliché in any culture, but in America it is almost an obligatory prescription for popular success. No American audience wants to read a story or see a movie where the hero does not achieve some kind of victory over adversity. Even sad songs should be easily recognisable tales of true love lost or found. Such audiences would also prefer a hero who is heroic in their home country so that they can all somehow share in or at least identify with his triumph. As Mort himself once said when he was exploring a very different style of song writing in Europe, 'America wanted love songs. They didn't want songs about old people and prostitutes and wars and the human condition'.

Both Pomus and Shuman were born in Brooklyn but in contrast with Doc's life which was lived almost exclusively in the New York area, Mort's successes were international and multi-cultural. He seemed to learn foreign languages without even trying. He loved Paris more than New York, and London more than Paris but became a major star in France, wrote musicals, wrote movie soundtracks and acted in movies. In his European years he recorded songs about awkward real life for grown-ups, not adolescent self-pity. Everyone he worked with seemed to find him a warm and generous collaborator as well as enormous fun... even Doc Pomus who admittedly had the misfortune of working with Mort in his irresponsible youth. Yet it was during that irresponsible youth that Mort Shuman wrote the music for a clutch of songs that helped define the popular music of the late 1950s and early 1960s. He never met one of Pomus-Shuman's greatest benefactors, Elvis Presley, but once said, 'When people tell me because of the songs I wrote I am part of the story, I just sit there and listen. But I say to myself: perhaps it's true'. If Mort left an international trail of broken hearts exacerbated by his tendency to ship out when romances went bad, in the end he married a beautiful French woman, fathered their daughters and ended his all-too-brief years a happy denizen of London. He died much too young but lived half a dozen colourful lives before he went.

Only the French ever issued a collection of recordings where the billing was Shuman & Pomus, not Pomus & Shuman. I would not want to go that far – to do so would be to rewrite history – but I hope this book goes at least some way toward rebalancing what for a few extraordinary years became an equal partnership between two quite brilliant Brooklynites separated in age by over eleven years, a grizzled blues shouter and a precocious young musician who came together for half a dozen years or so, wrote songs that sold over 30 million records, and then went their separate ways.

1

When Brooklyn Was The World

In any successful professional partnership, especially in the field of music, there is usually a potent third force. That force is often the 'and' or the ampersand in the partnership's name. That simple conjunction sometimes turns a creative duo into something magically more than the sum of its two parts. Frequently it also proves to be the seed of the collaboration's eventual destruction. It is as though each partner eventually comes to resent the other because it can seem to them that alone neither of them was quite good enough to make it without the efforts of the other. Where big egos are involved, this can be an unwelcome thought. From Gilbert & Sullivan through to Lennon & McCartney there are countless examples that fit the pattern... and a few that do not.

Doc Pomus and Mort Shuman worked together as a startlingly successful song writing partnership for half a dozen years, and more patchily for another three or four. To a generation of young record buyers in the 1950s and 60s their names, linked beneath the title on a 45rpm vinyl single was a pretty exciting prospect. The music papers eventually revealed a few details about the New York team of Pomus-Shuman, although these rarely amounted to much more than the information that Doc Pomus, stricken with polio as a child, walked with crutches and Mort Shuman didn't. The music papers did not say so but the pair had got together for the most pragmatic reasons, ex-blues shouter Doc, already a bit too old and world-weary to be appealing to the teenage record buying public, took on the younger Morty to try to make a few bucks as a song writing team. Jerry Leiber and Mike Stoller had shown how it could be done – they even cut Pomus in on royalties for a song he had started to write, failed to finish and left with them to kick around. Mortie, a naturally gifted young musician, was up for anything and to begin with was only too happy to play the teenage apprentice to Doc's seasoned music pro. It hardly sounds like the classic pairing of two talents that would bring the best out of one another. Doc Pomus, his mobility restricted by his health and in possession of a salty, defensive and no-bullshit disposition, would simply never have seen it that way. A bluesman, he didn't even like pop music all that much and saw song writing mainly as a business opportunity in a world that for a severely disabled man like him held limited opportunities. Mortie, meanwhile, showed early signs of being a pleasure-seeker and traveller, unreliable but a passionate, talented and likable whizz-kid musician with a natural gift for languages who was always thinking about tomorrow. Yet they did have some things in common: both were Jewish and both adored black music. Perhaps the most significant link between them, however, was the place that they grew up: the New York borough of Brooklyn.

Separated in age by almost eleven-and-a-half years, Pomus and Shuman had grown up not far from one another in Brooklyn, the populous New York City borough that had always been home to immigrants. When they got together Pomus was already familiar with life on the other side of the East River, frequenting Manhattan's clubs, bars, dives and hotels with Bohemian gusto. Mortie would follow, eventually extending his travels all over the world. Despite their age gap both had grown up in the period between 1920 (when the subway came) and 1957 (when the totemic Brooklyn Dodgers finally left for California), both significant dates for the borough. The Brooklyn of that time frame housed a multi-racial society but it was no cosmopolitan Paris to which émigrés flocked in search of art, romance or retreat, but rather a roiling adjunct to Manhattan where the neighbourhoods shifted identities as ethnic fortunes fluctuated and Brooklyn's relationship with Manhattan grew ever closer in response to improving transport links.

Doc, real name Jerome Solon Felder, was born in Brooklyn's densely inhabited district of East Williamsburg on June 27, 1925. Williamsburg itself had started out as a village within the town of Bushwick in 1826, becoming a town in its own right in 1840 and achieving city status in 1852. Further realignments prompted by growth, an influx of wealth and the expanding transport links to Manhattan, resulted in Brooklyn becoming one of New York City's five boroughs in 1898, five years before the Williamsburg Bridge supplied the borough's grand project: a fixed link to Manhattan's Lower East Side.

In 1925 the Felder family's little patch of Williamsburg was on McKibbin Street at Manhattan Avenue, a mainly Jewish area although, as in most Brooklyn immigrant settlements, one that also housed other ethnicities, in this case mainly Irish and black families. The Felder family was effectively headed by Millie (née Goldstein), an immigrant from the East End of London who had entered the US through Ellis Island at the age of 15 and found work as a seamstress. She was a steely and aspirational woman, poor but with a highly developed work ethic, especially on her husband's behalf. She was a cousin of the British politician, Ian Mikardo, a Zionist and committed socialist who belonged to the left wing of the Labour party and in his younger days was a close working colleague of the party's future leader Michael Foot.

How much Millie knew about her cousin's gradual rise to fame in the service of the causes and principles he held dear is not clear but at the start of her marriage she certainly seemed to labour under a misplaced belief that in Moritz Felder she had found a go-getter who would confer prestige and a comfortable middle-class life on the family. Unfortunately her life in Brooklyn showed few early signs of shaping up as much of an improvement on what she had left behind on the Mile End Road in London. Moritz was Austrian immigrant who had also arrived via Ellis Island and whose dreams of wealth and position in which Millie had placed her trust were forever doomed to remain unrealised. Despite the poverty of his own upbringing in Vienna, Moritz had originally trained as a veterinary surgeon, a profession which might have proved worthwhile in Austria but which turned out to be entirely redundant in this neck of Brooklyn where pet ownership did not flourish if it existed at all. Aiming higher he enrolled in law school but was never able to make any money from the practice he subsequently set up. As status and wealth continued to elude him he continued to aim high, seeing himself as a potential statesman, to which eventual end he became a dogged participant in the field of local politics, effectively hi-jacking the local Democratic society and campaigning for passionately-held but often quixotic causes while running for every public office going. He lost almost all of these social battles and bids for office with a regularity that seems almost statistically unlikely. State senator, assemblyman, judge – all were applied for and all were denied him. One triumph was his petition concerning the reinstatement of one of baseball's few Jewish players whom the iconic local team, The Brooklyn Dodgers, had demoted to the minor leagues. However the only office he ever held was as that of assistant counsel to the Transport Department. He was a disappointment to himself as well as to his wife, and his lack of success and social influence was a genuine misfortune since he was a passionate and selfless believer in social justice but simply seemed to lack the charisma and personality to rise to any position of power and influence.

Millie's hopes of a better life based on Moritz's once promising ambition were further eroded as the McKibbin Street apartment filled up with political leaflets and extended family members among whom soon featured her retired and widowed father Harris Goldstein, an elderly skirt-chaser who had joined them from London with the rather unrealistic ambition of pursuing the life of a snappily-dressed *boulevardier* who expected to be supported by Millie and Moritz. He energetically supported his daughter in her regular tirades against Moritz who was now known as Morris and remained as far away as ever from achieving his dreams as an influential Democratic politician. In his wife's eyes, he was not even a reliable breadwinner. Soured by Millie's chronic disillusionment, the household into which Jerome Felder was born in 1925 would prove a tense place in which to grow up, a place perennially spiked with bitter rows and hostile silences.

The 1920s saw parts of Williamsburg, along with other nearby neighbourhoods, rapidly increase in population. Around half a million people moved to Brooklyn during the decade and by the time of The Depression many parts had become if not gentrified at least heavily built up. Not for the first time Brooklyn was reinventing itself and despite the tensions and parental hostility of home life, the young Jerome was not short of entertainment and diversion, much of it musical. He would have no siblings until he was fourteen years old when a brother, Raoul Lionel, was born, but he was a lively and feisty kid who particularly revelled in annual visits to the beach. Meanwhile his grandfather Harris – who could be quite amiable in between his vituperative broadsides of moral support for his daughter – would sometimes take him to vaudeville matinees at a the Folly Theater, an aptly named domed architectural confection at the junction of Brooklyn's Debevoise Street and Graham Avenue where music acts performed on a bill alongside comedians, ventriloquists and dancers.

The Felders, still far from rich, would nonetheless rent a summer bungalow at Manhattan Beach where, until the age of seven, Jerome would actively enjoy the sand and the sea as well as the music performances held at a band shell at the Brighton Beach Baths. Brooklyn's proximity to the island of Manhattan meant that there was no shortage of big names. Just as The Folly's vaudeville had featured nationally famous ventriloquist Ed Bergen, Brighton Beach Baths routinely served up well-known acts like the renowned bandleader of the 30s, Paul Whiteman. Although Jerome's memory later suffered from blanking out much of his life that preceded the health trauma that would strike him at the age of seven, it was reliably reported that on one occasion he ran up on stage during Whiteman's set and insisted on singing and dancing along; his chutzpah earned him a one-off appearance on a children's radio show about which he later remembered little, possibly due to terror. The Whiteman stage invasion would not be the last time the young Jerome Felder would push himself forward as an impromptu performer, although the next occasion would be in the face of terrible odds and would change his life forever.

Jerome's life took a dramatic turn for the worse when, like many other children in the first half of the 20th century, he contracted poliomyelitis. A crippling disease that had been around forever, it reached its modern-day height during the epidemic of 1952 which saw nearly 60,000 cases and 3,000 deaths recorded in the US alone. The virus would be completely eliminated in the Western hemisphere by 1991 but before then it was the real stuff of nightmares for parents. Jerome contracted it in the summer of 1932, the time of his seventh birthday, when New York was in the grip of an epidemic. His parents had sent him to a country camp in Connecticut far removed from the disease's epicentre but he succumbed while he was there, losing the feeling in his legs. It was a quite devastating affliction which would transform and restrict the remainder of his life.

Brought back to Brooklyn by his distraught parents, Jerome saw his own future reflected in the faces of fellow sufferers at a local hospital which was the first port of call. Doctors were consulted but in truth there was little to be done. Jonas Salk, another child of Jewish immigrants in New York, was a brilliant medical researcher whose discovery of a polio vaccine in 1955 came too late for Jerome's generation of afflicted children but would mark the beginning of the eradication of polio in most of the developed world. The disease that had terrified American parents would wreak one more catastrophic epidemic in 1952 which was mercifully the last in the country. Not all who contracted polio suffered the withered and weakened limbs characteristic of the most serious cases, and perhaps because of this it was once often assumed that exercise and healthy environments might stave off or minimise the worst effects. In fact the extent of damage depended almost entirely on the path of invasiveness of the virus. Many well-known people (including Joni Mitchell, Donald Sutherland and Francis Coppola) contracted it without serious physical after-effects although British rocker Ian Dury, who fell victim aged seven in a 1949 British outbreak, suffered a shrivelled hand and leg. Ironically, one of the most celebrated polio sufferers, a man whose personality and favourite place of treatment were to touch on the Felder family, may not have had the disease at all. Franklin D. Roosevelt went to great lengths always to be photographed seated so that voters would not be aware of his incapacity, but eventually it became public knowledge (or at least belief) that he suffered from polio. If he did, he contracted it unusually late in life (age 39) and this has led to a retrospective re-assessment that favours a diagnosis of Guillain–Barre syndrome.

Young Jerome Felder was sent to Roosevelt's own spa, Warm Springs in Georgia, in the autumn of 1932. Roosevelt had acquired it in 1929 and set up a second home nearby that would become known as The Little White House. The veracity of family stories about Jerome seeing FDR languishing in Warm Springs restorative waters and Millie Felder actually being been bitten by the great man's terrier remains a matter of conjecture. However, since in November of 1932 New York's Roosevelt would win an historic victory, defeating Herbert Hoover for the presidency, it seems appropriate that any brush, however tenuous, with the crippled Democratic president whose party Morris had laboured so tirelessly to support, should become part of the Felder family history.

Jerome's Georgia sojourn in the aura of a famous politician was followed by a much grimmer experience back in New York State where he was consigned to the joyless Rehabilitation Home in the Town of Haverstraw, Rockland County. It seems that the prevailing wisdom of the day was that polio-stricken children needed to be toughened up (and Pomus' abrasive institutional experiences certainly sound similar to those of Ian Dury some 17 years later in the south of England).

Emotional support was an unknown concept, cure was impossible and basic surgery was ineffectual but arbitrarily essayed, usually resulting in rigid limbs being locked into what was deemed a more practical geometry than before. The proximity of fellow sufferers was more likely to result in bullying than solidarity, and by the time Jerome left the Haverstraw facility equipped with leg brace and crutches, he had already begun to withdraw into a world of isolation, dispossession and suppressed aggression. He was now two years older than when he first contracted the virus and his immediate prospect was further isolation, bedridden at home. Millie and Morris changed apartments to take up residence around the corner on Manhattan Avenue in a building with a lift – a rarity in the neighbourhood – to accommodate Jerome's disability. The once active child was now forced to stay indoors for much of the time, venturing out with the help of crutches and leg braces which, when growing up, he would always try to disguise if a family photograph was being taken. This resulted in snapshots of him leaning against a storefront wall, a column or some other support, in various attitudes of defiant instability. His amusements were no longer the physically exuberant ones of street games or annual beach visits, but cerebral flights of fancy fed by adventure stories in books and music and drama on the radio.

In those pre-TV days American radio was an all-powerful medium offering plays, news and most significantly a cornucopia of richly varied music with many local variations. For a growing boy with an active mind, a love of music and no distractions in the shape of outdoor recreations, the radio stations served up a priceless feast of musical genres: classical, the light popular music of the day, show tunes, big band and more. Jerome absorbed them all but his epiphany came when he discovered black music. Its visceral power and persuasiveness hit him before he learned anything about its categorisation into subgenres. As he trawled the stations he knew that this music held the key and would offer him a soundtrack to his new unsought life as an outsider suddenly denied many of the opportunities he might once have expected.

Jazz and swing grabbed him but the blues electrified him. He became obsessed with the sound of the saxophone and persuaded his parents to let him have lessons. At the age of ten he was still in a kind of limbo, his only formal education consisting of examination papers sporadically delivered and completed with indeterminate results. Vocational training came in the form of two summer courses, in 1937 and 1938, conducted at a physical therapy facility in Far Rockaway in the southern part of the neighbouring borough of Queens. There he studied mechanical drawing in a desultory fashion but was most struck with the contrast between the prison-like confines of the facility and the tempting glimpses of the boardwalk beyond with its promenading beach-goers. The tactlessness of this juxtaposition – penned-in young invalids with a clear view of healthy pleasure-seekers – made escape, even temporary escape, a priority. Not for the last time music was to prove the key to freedom when Jerome joined an amateur band of fellow inmates who were allowed to perform on the boardwalk. His level of accomplishment on the saxophone was limited, and the prescribed marching band repertoire bore no resemblance to the thrilling sounds of The Fletcher Henderson Orchestra he had heard on the radio, but the experience of belonging to a small group of outsiders who could win a reprieve from confinement through music left a lasting impression.

In the summer of the following year, 1939, he would be 14 and instead of sending him to Far Rockaway yet again his parents, now with new baby Raoul who had been born in May, enrolled Jerome in Bushwick High School, to start in the ninth grade that September.

The prospects for a disabled and inexperienced teenage loner at a rough Brooklyn high school were not good. Unsurprisingly, once there he developed an aggressive manner and mordant wit as defence mechanisms against teasing, insults and rejection. Despite his high

IQ, the only lesson that did not bore him was music. His future was simultaneously unguessable and assured. He had little in common with his is quarrelsome parents. His soul mates had never been his fellow polio sufferers and they would not be found among his high school peers either. Brooklyn was where he had been born and raised but he felt his spiritual homeland lay across the East River in Manhattan, in a sprawling neighbourhood that spanned the island for some fifty blocks north of Central Park. It would be two years before The Glenn Miller Orchestra released a song whose title perfectly fitted the young fantasist's dream.

2

I Dreamt I Was In Harlem

Mortimer Shuman was born on November 12 in 1938 in a Brooklyn district that ten-year-old Jerome Felder must have envied when he made childhood summer visits: Brighton Beach. The Oceanside neighbourhood was referred to by Shuman in his 1991 jottings for a never-to-be completed autobiography as once having been 'the Deauville of New York' even though its name, bestowed in 1896, was intended to evoke the English seaside resort in Sussex. Like Felder, Shuman was the child of émigré European Jews, Louis Shulman and Esther Drucker who had arrived, separately and unknown to each other, from Warsaw, Poland. (It is not clear at what point in Louis' assimilation into the United States 'Shulman' became 'Shuman' although the original name may have been briefly handed on to Mortimer.)

Mortimer's version of his parents' history makes it sound like the plot of an 18th century novel, all colourful drama, death and wild coincidence. It is a background that may go some way towards explaining one or two of the recurring themes in Mortimer Shuman's own life such as an addiction to travel and recurring instances of relationships ended by tactical relocation.

It seems that Louis Shulman, a factory worker, thought it wise to depart Warsaw in 1920 after killing a German officer. Setting sail for The United States he left behind a wife and three children to be summoned later. It was not a journey without diversion. Fetching up penniless in Glasgow, Louis found work with a Jewish barber and was even tempted to stay in the city having taken a liking to his employer's daughter. In the end, whether out of discretion, fidelity or other motives, Louis decided against a life in Scotland and pressed on to New York.

Meanwhile a young woman by the name of Esther Drucker was also fated to leave Warsaw in fraught circumstances. She had been secretly engaged to a man called Max whose mother's controlling nature apparently posed major problems for all her family members, both existing and prospective. Perhaps because of the insurmountable problem of turning a secret engagement into a secret marriage, Esther and Max's betrothal was abruptly terminated. Almost at once broken-hearted Esther found herself leaving Poland in the company of her parents, two sisters and two brothers, clutching a photograph of her beloved but now lost Max, and bound for New York along with many other Jewish families seeking to escape the growing threat of persecution at home.

After processing at Ellis Island, Esther and her family settled in a Jewish ghetto on the lower East Side of Manhattan. The prevailing culture was the conventional one of attempting to recreate something of the homeland in a tiny pocket of an unfamiliar country. After a few months, at one of the many neighbourhood parties thrown to alleviate homesickness, Esther was dumbfounded to spot a man she instantly took to be her ex- fiancé. It was in fact Louis Shulman who bore a startling resemblance to her lost love Max and she rushed over to him impelled by what turned out to be a case of mistaken identity. Esther omitted to tell Louis him why she had first seemed so familiar and then confused... at least until after they had gradually become close and she finally admitted her mistake. An astonished Louis revealed that he actually had a brother called Max back in Poland.

Esther produced her treasured photograph and the coincidence was confirmed. Soon Louis decided to divorce by proxy in order to marry Esther, a not unusual procedure at the time. For the new couple the union was an improbably happy twist of fate; for others it would have awful ramifications. The family Louis never summoned remained in Poland and his first wife and their youngest child would die in the camps.

Like Morris Felder, Louis and Esther came from a militant working community and in the new country helped to form The International Workers Order (IWO), an organisation that came into being after a split between two other bodies. It combined the provision of low cost and non-discriminatory insurance with Communist-leaning principles. Eventually The IWO would fall foul of the Special Committee on Un-American Activities of the US House of Representatives, but in the early days its progressive social programme was widely seen as a benign social service created by and for the dispossessed.

As the Shumans (or Shulmans) gained better jobs they left the ghetto and over a period of time moved into a succession of larger, better appointed apartments, first in the Bronx then in Brooklyn. Eventually they found one on the top floor of a house in a tree-lined street close to the sea in Brighton Beach. The district's so-called Deauville days were already long gone but Brighton Beach, with its boardwalk and ocean breezes, was still a significant improvement on Manhattan's Lower East Side where the two refugees had started out. After more than a dozen years together, in 1936 the patient Shumans decided the time was at last right to have a child.

Mortimer was born into a microcosm that, many years later and a continent away, he would re-imagine as Brooklyn by the Sea in one of his French language songs. In Brighton Beach Yiddish was the community mother tongue, English being reserved for talking to the teacher or filling out forms. His parents remained progressive if not radical in their politics and in this they were very much in tune with the local community which Mortimer later likened to a seaside *shtetl*

13

– a small Jewish town or village of the sort found dotted throughout Eastern Europe before WW2.

Esther and Louis sang in the Community Choir and Louis played in a Mandolin Orchestra. There were readings in people's homes and Saturday night get-togethers on the boardwalk during the summer featuring traditional food and impromptu music that included fiddle-playing and singing.

American-born Mortimer spoke only Yiddish until the age of five although later – indeed quite soon – he would start to become fluent in a startling number of languages. When growing up, however, English was his second language and he learned it in elementary school in the early 1940s.

★   ★   ★

Jerome Felder's belated start at Bushwick High in late 1939 continued to reinforce his growing feeling of always being the wrong person in the wrong place. His disability could simply not be ignored even in the best of situations and, magnified by the abrasive and cliquey nature of high school life, it appeared to destine him for a life of isolation and victimisation. He clung to music lessons like a life raft and his music teacher, a local bandleader, taught him to sight-read as well as write harmonies and arrangements. Jerome's personal badge of excellence was the alto sax he wore slung around his neck even when he was not playing it in the school band. In truth his skill on the instrument was hardly exceptional but the instrument's real value lay in being a highly visible talisman testifying to his special talent. Music, in some shape or form, seemed to be presenting itself as an escape route, perhaps, somehow, even as a career.

Unconvivial Millie and Morris took a more traditional view of the chances of the saxophone offering a plausible way of making a living for their disabled elder son. On the other hand for the time being they could see little harm in his participating in the military-style school band. Jerome, however, had found a second kindred spirit in the music class and she had other ideas. It was a fellow student, one Mary Barget, a self-possessed girl who wanted to explore musical territory beyond John Philip Souza and saw in Jerome a potential ally. She became a friend and supporter, recognising the bond of music between them. The place to play, she said, was a Brooklyn dive called The Lincoln Cabaret where she had been assured by the bartender, with whom she seemed to enjoy some sort of relationship, that they might play and get paid. Augmented with two other music students they did just that. Jerome did not tell Millie and Morris who would no doubt have felt the conventional alarm of most parents presented with the prospect of a teenager from a decent family working in a place with an informal attitude towards liquor, drugs and girls. Instead Jerome offered them a vague and serviceable alibi that involved visiting his Brooklyn cousins Bernard and Max.

The band not only got paid as promised, it got return engagements. What was more, thanks to resourceful Mary, an additional gig was arranged at a family-friendly deli on Broadway. So it was that the Felder clan one day turned out to see Jerome and the band playing in a venue that was in every sense kosher. This in turn took the pressure off Jerome's heavy reliance on excuses that he was visiting with his cousins when actually playing at the Lincoln Cabaret. Bernard and Max, sons of Millie's sister, were slightly eccentric allies but Jerome anyway preferred their company as a regular respite from the warring atmosphere of home life. Quite how long he could use them as an alibi on band nights still remained uncertain but the possibility now emerged that he could at least claim to be playing in respectable places.

Meanwhile he remained the kind of fan for whom the music is a drug, not a pastime. Many years later he recalled: "The first records I bought were 'Traffic Jam' by Artie Shaw and 'Scatterbrain' by Freddy Martin. I bought them in a neighborhood record bin for five cents. I liked the trumpet sections and the saxophone sections of an orchestra."

In 1941 at the age of 16 Jerome had his Damascene moment in a local record store called Lineker's when he came across a Big Joe Turner record. It opened up another world for him, one for which fate already seemed to have been somehow preparing him, however imperfectly. Jerome sensed that music was both his escape and the way ahead but so far his alto sax playing had not made him confident of his own ability to become an exceptional musician or even a particularly good one.

Big Joe Turner was blues shouter whose real name – Joseph Vernon Turner Jr. – had been reduced to a snappy stage moniker and whose big voice, it would turn out, was more than matched by a huge physical presence. That voice had already distilled all the power of the blues into the grooves of the second-hand 78 rpm Decca record Jerome bought that day: 'Piney Brown Blues'. Jerome later discovered that Piney Brown was the picturesque soubriquet of Walter Brown, a Kansas City club owner who had once employed Joe Turner as a bartender. At a stroke the example of Turner revolutionised Jerome Felder's life and dreams. "When I heard Joe Turner... my life changed," he acknowledged. "That's how I felt singing should be, that's how I felt music should be."

'The Boss Of The Blues', as his new idol was also known (Turner even sported a business card bearing that job description and the words 'Available for Clubs, Concerts, Parties, Television, Radio'), would play 'Piney Brown Blues' throughout his long career which spanned a performing partnership with boogie-woogie stars Albert Ammons and Meade Lux Lewis in the late 1930s, and the creation of a body of work that laid the blues foundations for white rock'n'roll in the 1950s. In fact Big Joe Turner would record rock'n'roll staple 'Shake, Rattle and Roll' in 1954 before Bill Haley & His Comets and Elvis Presley got hold of it, but back in 1941 in Lineker's record store Big Joe Turner was nothing more or less than the portentous voice of The Blues... and, the blues was suddenly Jerome's world. Fourteen years later Turner would actually record a Jerome Felder song, but that would only come after the teenage fan had made something of a career out of being a blues shouter himself.

The transition from sax player to vocalist was assisted – if that is the word – by a street assault that fractured several bones in Jerome's right hand. The hand never healed properly and left him with nerve damage that prevented him from fingering the keys of the instrument at which he had never excelled anyway. In any case his band's tenure at the Lincoln Cabaret ended after some altercation between the bartender and Mary Barget. It seemed that disasters large and small were conspiring to push him towards what he really wanted to do. When bedridden at home as he often was, Jerome had become accustomed to bellowing for his mother, a necessity which he now started to use to develop his lungs, shouting fragments of 'Piney Brown Blues' lyrics along with his more mundane requests. Wondering if he would he ever get to sound like Turner was another of the teasing notions that filled his dreams of an unattainable fantasy life which he would later describe in a personal journal entry from 1982.

"I would get out of the wheelchair and walk and not with braces and crutches…. young girls in see-through dresses would smile at me… I would always sing and everybody would always love to hear me…."

Jerome Felder was aware that in his fantasising he was not entirely alone. Other cruelly dispossessed men and women had a dream too and they were held back not by withered limbs but by the colour of their skin. In Big Joe Turner, Jerome had acquired a defining role model who was neither Jewish nor white. The writer Norman Mailer was both, and in the summer of 1957 he would publish an essay called *The White Negro: Superficial Reflections On The Hipster* in which he discussed the phenomenon of young white people of the 1920s, 1930s and 1940s who loved jazz, blues and swing music to such an extent that they embraced black culture as their own. Jewish jazzman Milton Mesirow (aka Mezz Mezzrow) had declared himself a 'voluntary Negro' in the 1920s and so became an early hero for the hipsters of the 1940s as well as the Beat Generation of the 1950s. For Jerome Felder, the role of outsider had been thrust upon him by arbitrary physical affliction; it was conspicuous and owed nothing to the sort of white adolescent self-dramatization that in 1955 would be personified by James Dean in the movie *Rebel Without A Cause*. In any case Jerome's spiritual brethren were not the white kids of Brooklyn and his music was not that of the bland pop vocalists on mainstream radio. He now identified fully with the blacks of Harlem and the heart-wrenching sound of the blues.

★　★　★

When Mortimer (now usually Mort or Mortie) Shuman progressed to High School it was Abraham Lincoln High in Coney Island. A hotbed of famous names over the years, the school was also attended at various times by movie actor Harvey Keitel, *Catch-22* author Joseph Heller, playwright Arthur Miller, singer Neil Diamond and fellow pop composers and contemporaries Neil Sedaka and Howard Greenfield. Before getting there Mort Shuman had enjoyed a vivid upbringing in Brighton Beach and its environs, playing an old guitar that his father bought him and singing in Yiddish, taking piano lessons and attending art school on Saturdays. His fiddle-playing Uncle Murray, who was rarely sober according to Mort, gave him a crash course in classical music while plying him with bourbon even though he was 'very young'. A precocious interest in marijuana may explain why most of Mort's accounts of his early teenage life tend to be sketchy, but the key points he identified were his refusal of bar-mitzvah on the grounds that he mistrusted all organized religion, and a burgeoning love of rhythm'n'blues music. If there was no single moment of epiphany like Jerome Felder's encounter with the Big Joe Turner record, Mort Shuman's conversion to black blues music was no less fervent or sincere. His spiritual opinions and carnal appetites modified by weed (and quite probably the start of a lifetime addiction to alcohol courtesy of Uncle Murray) he dismissed the white music on the radio and became a full-blooded R&B man. He even learned to play it on the piano and guitar.

★   ★   ★

Two years after buying that Big Joe Turner record Jerome Felder, for the second time in his life, thrust himself into the limelight by climbing onto a stage to perform – no easy task for him, emotionally or physically. The story goes that he had little choice since George's Tavern, the Greenwich Village jazz club where the teenager liked to lurk in the shadows while nursing a solitary drink all night, was not run by charitable men. One night one of the owners brusquely challenged him to spend money or leave to which Jerome responded, in a mixture of panic, bluster and ambition, by announcing that he was there to sing a song. There was no turning back. His song choice was, predictably enough, 'Piney Brown Blues'. The resident band led by trumpeter Frankie Newton (who had famously performed on records by Bessie Smith and Billie Holiday) now played the three chords it shared by innumerable other blues songs and Jerome gave it his all. There and then he became a blues shouter. There was some applause.

After the adrenaline came the career plan. Some accounts have Jerome returning to George's the very next night already equipped with the stage name Doc Pomus. More plausibly he spent some time working on what he saw as the all-important name that outwardly would sound right in the smoky subterranean clubs where he saw his future career unfolding, and, more intimately, would be the personal symbol of the triumphant self-reinvention of Jerome Felder, the crippled Jewish high school nobody. The timetable of events is less important than the outcome which was that the newly-christened Doc Pomus would for a time become a regular performer at George's where, scarcely believably, he would soon be backed by the first of several big name jazz and bluesmen who sat in at the Greenwich Village club from time to time. Jerome/Doc had already begun his blues singing career in front of Frankie Newton (whose name the distinguished British Marxist historian Eric Hobsbawm borrowed for his *nom de plume* when reviewing jazz for *The New Statesman* magazine). Soon afterwards, still at the age of 18, he would be backed onstage by the legendary tenor saxophonist and clarinetist Lester Young, late of the Count Basie band.

He rapidly expanded his repertoire, learning other songs from records and writing his own blues song, suitably personalised – Doc's BB Blues' had nothing to do with BB King, but instead referred to Brighton Beach, the summer destination he had loved as a child. 'Piney Brown Blues', with its evocative first line so memorably savoured in that record store ('Well I've been to Kansas City/Girls and everything is really alright') was of course a Doc Pomus staple. Things were moving fast. He developed a taste for marijuana and whiskey. For the time being, Doc was the pathfinder, one of what Norman Mailer had yet to dub White Negroes. In a few years Mort would become one too, before he ever met Doc, propelled, by his own admission, both by musical predisposition and the enthusiastic consumption of weed. Rejecting the bland radio pop music of Perry Como and Jo Stafford as 'white crap' Mort must nonetheless have felt a twinge of recognition in the title of the radio hit from white Glenn Miller: 'I Dreamt I Lived In Harlem'. Doc's Joe Turner anthem, 'Piney Brown Blues', contained the line 'I dreamed last night/I was standing on Eighteenth and Vine'. With an 11-year age difference and possessing very different temperaments, Doc and Mort would share the same dream. All that remained was for that age difference to be eroded (Mort would have been about five years old when Doc first hobbled onto the stage at George's Tavern) and for them to meet. It would be ten years before that happened.

3

The Doctor Pays His Dues

The first meeting between Doc and Mort would not take place until around 1954. Doc was approaching thirty and Mort was sixteen. It would not have taken place at all but for the most casually fortuitous of reasons and it would take a while for them to get one other's measure. With hindsight their age gap, like many another, seems flexible by nature: a chasm in youth, increasingly narrower in adulthood. From today's perspective another distorting factor is that physically ravaged Doc, overweight, eventually wheelchair-bound and a lifelong smoker, would die in New York in the same year that adventurer and *bon viveur* Mort would pass away in London. Mort barely had time to write Doc's obituary for a music magazine. That biographical coincidence seems to conspire with the duo's extraordinary decade-long song writing partnership to cast them as contemporaries in the popular imagination. Never, though, was their age discrepancy more significant than between the years of 1943 to 1954 when Jerome-by-day/Doc-by-night laboured to reconcile the awkward and painful realities of the day-to-day world with the edgy nocturnal pleasures of singing the blues in the black clubs of Manhattan, Brooklyn and New Jersey while Mortie was going through elementary school and then high school where he embarked on a moody adolescence.

With what might seem surprising practicality, in the year of his first modest success as a singer, Jerome had left Bushwick High School and enrolled in Brooklyn College to major in political science. The move, he felt, would placate his parents. Millie was showing ominous signs of being zealous about getting him to settle down in one of the restricted number of jobs she believed his condition might permit. In reality Brooklyn College's appeal for him lay in its social life where, in his new guise as a night-shift working jazzman, he was more accepted than he had ever been at high school. The college had a jazz club too and since no other students had his kind of qualification to be its president, it was a role he soon assumed.

Sex, or its likely scarcity, had always been one of Jerome's most deep-seated concerns and according to his journals his dreams were still populated with idealistic illusions about life, music and, especially, impossibly available girls. Now he was starting to attract the real thing, the first college candidate being one Barbara Silver in whom were combined pretty looks and a genuine love of jazz.

Like so much in Jerome's life, biddable Barbara Silver was to prove something of a false dawn. She seemed – and probably was – sincere in her affection for him. Indeed she actively encouraged him to come in and meet her parents but Jerome's dread of their reaction to seeing their daughter with someone on crutches and wearing leg braces always made him decline. For his part he never invited her to the increasingly dangerous clubs in which he sang. His roster was now starting to take in Brooklyn joints which he found he often preferred to the Greenwich Village or mid-town Manhattan venues where the clientèle was predominantly white and often out slumming or inclined towards pseudo-intellectual analysis of the music. Eventually he and Barbara drifted apart without ever having had sex and when Jerome discovered that she had subsequently been seduced by his cousin Max it was another major disappointment to add to the many others that would accrue over the years. She eventually married someone else by which time Doc had dropped out of Brooklyn College, mainly because the only time he felt complete was on stage in some smoky black club in Greenwich Village or Harlem or Brooklyn or across the Hudson in Newark.

He did pretty well in those risky, smoky dives, getting plenty of work on the informal circuit, although he remained unsure what the black patrons and musicians thought of a white blues singer. Impersonator? Satirist? Eccentric? Doc knew he was a rarity although it was more likely that he was unique. He gave it all he had and for a few years that was enough. During that period spanning much of the 1940s and the early 1950s he became something a local hero for many who saw him perform in the clubs and bars. The denizens of those clubs owed absolutely nothing to the roguish but basically lovable demi-monde characters of Damon Runyon's Broadway stories. On the contrary these were often desperate people on the fringes of society and frequently in between the prison sentences that represented the only formal structure in their lives. Danger was a familiar part of such places and while Doc met plenty of women, they were usually available only at a price which might come in anywhere between a few bucks and a violent reprisal from the man she forgot to mention. A recurring pattern would emerge, alternating highs and lows of improbably lucky breaks with mean personal betrayals. As a result the young self-appointed bluesman was increasingly treading the thin line between scepticism and cynicism, his low expectations sometimes becoming self-fulfilling prophecies. Doc still needed his own heroes and a new one came along in the compact form of Little Jimmy Scott who soon joined Big Joe Turner (there seemed to be no blues singers of medium stature… at least none who wished to advertise the fact in their stage name) in Doc's personal list of favourites.

Cleveland-born Scott was exactly the same age as Doc and had his own burden to bear in the form of arrested physical development that left him in a permanent pre-pubertal state, small of stature and with a very high-pitched voice. As a singer he was extraordinary and would soon record a vocal hit with The Lionel Hampton Band

('Everybody's Somebody's Fool', for which he received no credit) and another ('Embraceable You' with Charlie Parker) on which he was mis-identified as a female vocalist. Doc first met Jimmy in a Harlem club, struck up a friendship and showed him the best places to eat and drink in Manhattan before introducing him to the Brooklyn blues circuit. Perhaps surprisingly Doc had not cut off ties with the Brooklyn of his warring parents and his own traumatic childhood affliction. Never having valued the borough much, neither did he particularly feel the need to escape from it. He even came to prefer the down-and-dirty black clubs centred on its Bedford Stuyvesant district to their Manhattan and Newark counterparts. He later recalled that The Elks Club on Fulton Street was the biggest of the Brooklyn clubs and featured a kind of funky vaudeville bill on which he was always welcome; the roughest was The Cobra Club in Brownsville with a reputation for trouble that necessitated a ranked boxer taking on the role of bouncer.

With Jimmy he would still venture to Harlem just to hear others perform and that was where he met Billie Holiday who was herself a solid Little Jimmy Scott fan. Jimmy also introduced Doc to his brother's stepdaughter, the exotic Aida Scott whose beauty suggested a cocktail of Arab and African American ancestry. She too was a singer with her own uniquely jazzy flavoured soprano that defied classification. She fell for Doc and they had an affair although the increasingly hard-bitten young blues shouter had by now been disappointed too many times fully to give himself to her – or indeed to anyone. Jimmy, Aida and Doc hung out together, often crossing the Hudson to Newark to visit Cookie's Caravan, a magnet for some great blues singers. Among them was Andrew Tibbs, a man whose name is today largely forgotten, perhaps because his appeal lay more in live performance than recording.

Tibbs (born Melvin Grayson in Columbus, Ohio) was a politically-motivated bluesman, his first record being a celebration of the death of racist politician Theodore G. Bilbo, 'Bilbo Is Dead'. Tibbs and Doc occasionally appeared on the same bill and liked to do a blues-

24

style duel, each trying to out-shout the other. It was ironic that Andrew Tibbs and his brother Kenneth would in a few years' time record an early Pomus-Shuman novelty number ('[Wake Up] Miss Rip Van Winkle') for Atlantic which surely satisfied neither the serious-minded Andrew Tibbs nor the inchoate song writing team who rightly suspected that penning this kind of material was never going to make them rich. For now Doc's windswept life as a fan and performer of the blues made for a lively time and was the source of a lifetime of outrageous anecdotes, frequently exaggerated to such a degree that Doc himself sometimes forgot what was true and what was embellishment. His journal notes, written long after the events, are heavy with shaggy dog stories and stories of scams but light on emotional recollections except for accounts of his dreams about being loved and desired in a world where he was free from his disability. Aida, whom Doc had rather roughly cast as his blues shouter's moll, left town and soon enough he missed her.

He carried on, still dropping in on his parents from time to time, availing himself of food and laundry services and yet another helping of their indestructible marital hostility which time had in no way softened. In Manhattan home was a series of rented rooms in cheap hotels, often The Stratford Arms at 117 West 70th Street.

$\star \quad \star \quad \star$

The pattern varied little. He sang. He wrote the odd song. He recorded occasionally, although very few of his records had ever been played on radio or widely released. Recording was something many musicians did in New York, part of the routine, but without a major label or distributor it was not seen as anything special. The exception was Doc's first session because it offered tangible proof (in the form of a boxful of records) that he really was a blues singer, not the imposter he sometimes feared himself to be. It came about in October 1945 when British jazz critic Leonard Feather spotted Doc at the Pied Piper, another Greenwich Village club where occasionally Doc sang, occasionally accompanied by the young Milt Jackson. Feather, who was also a blues songwriter, invited Doc to record a couple of his own songs for the Apollo label. Doc sang with the Tab Smith Septette and the songs were 'Blues In The Red' and 'Blues Without Booze', still available nearly 70 years later on compilations of Doc's blues shouter years. If Brooklyn was by now only just hanging on to its reputation as The World, it remained in close touch with the famous, the soon-to-be famous and the once-famous. Doc often brushed shoulders with some of them.

He met Otis Blackwell, another Brooklynite, who combined a love of R&B with a taste for country music and would soon find fame as a songwriter for Elvis Presley, at which point he would give up his day job at a local tailor shop. Blackwell introduced Doc to his manager, Willie Saunders, whose subsequent efforts on behalf of both of them never produced any worthwhile paydays, so Doc pressed on with his song writing, usually trying to expand the kind of raw and repetitive blues he liked to sing with some twist he hoped might make the number stand out. He preferred to sing rather than write but Atlantic Records handled only black artists so Doc would write a few songs that were demo'd there, often without finding an artist or achieving a release. (When at last he did hit paydirt, in 1956, the taker would be none less that Ray Charles.)

He laboured on in what even he could now see was going to be a limited performing career. He struck up a relationship with one Constance Ockelman, another Brooklyn native, who he remembered first encountering in a local club in the early 1950s. She was in no better shape than many of the women who hung around the local bars and clubs even though, astonishingly, she had been one of the world's most famous women in the previous decade. As Veronica Lake she had made a triumphant debut in Preston Sturges' sublime movie *Sullivan's Travels* and seemingly cemented her stardom in *This Gun For Hire* with Alan Ladd. Her hairstyle had been even more famous than she was, featuring a curtain of tresses that obscured one eye; it was called the Peek-a-Boo or simply The Veronica Lake and made her famous all over the world, even for people who had never been to any of her movies but saw 'The Veronica Lake' pictured in magazines. Schizophrenia and alcoholism took hold and she never recovered her former success.* Sometimes the story is that Doc and Constance had an affair, other times their meeting is portrayed as nothing more than two damaged Brooklyn natives drinking together at some half-forgotten smoky bar – exactly which one even Doc never even pretended to remember. Once more, though, Doc, who rarely travelled outside the orbit of the local blues clubs, had shared a few drinks with someone who had briefly enjoyed worldwide fame.

Doc even met Duke Ellington when his second manager Maele Bartholomew (wife of former child star Freddie Bartholomew) booked him to front for Duke at a club called Murphy's in Elizabethtown, New Jersey. Regular gigs were also promised there but at first the thrilling prospect of working with Ellington was enough for Doc. It was just as well. Any possibility that Maele might prove more reliable than Willie Saunders would have been a triumph of hope over expectation. She proved a terrible manager who left Doc out of pocket (she once tried and failed to pay him off with heroin) and then left him stranded for the summer of 1950 living in a room above Murphy's with a showgirl whose love life followed the now familiar pattern of playing off men against one another. The girl broke off her summer dalliance with Doc by hitting him over the head with a bottle, always a sure sign that a relationship is not going well. If Doc needed further ill omens – and he didn't – the owner of Murphy's died when his car hit a tombstone.

In 1951 he actually met his idol Big Joe Turner at the Atlantic office and 'The Boss Of The Blues' – who had just seen Doc perform

---

* To introduce a personal note, I saw a rather tragic 1969 performance of *A Streetcar Named Desire* at a small provincial English theatre with Veronica Lake playing Blanche DuBois in a last ditch bid to recapture something of her former fame. Her casting as a once beautiful woman descending into madness seemed insensitive rather than apt. She was to die four years later.

at a club called The Harlem Baby Grand, turned out to be warm and encouraging, even asking Doc to write some material for him. Never more motivated to create, Doc wrote him a smoky ballad 'Still In Love' and 'Boogie Woogie Country Girl' (a nod towards The Andrews Sisters' 1941 hit 'Boogie Woogie Bugle Boy'). Still preferring singing to writing, Doc nevertheless took keen pleasure in supplying material to Turner and subsequently always tried to meet up with him at Atlantic Records when he knew his hero would be there.

★   ★   ★

For Doc during the first half of the 1950s, good fortune and disappointment seemed to follow one another with the inevitability of the seasons. Maele Bartholomew soon disappeared, leaving him without a manager again. He still left the odd song with Atlantic Records hoping that one day one would be picked up by a major artist. While he was undergoing his protracted and abrasive apprenticeship in the music, his future song writing partner Mort Shuman had been having a comparatively easy time growing up in Brighton Beach. His colourful family and friends – his whole *shtetl* in fact – had conspired to shower him with random culture, saturate him with home-made music, and stimulate what must surely have been some extraordinary innate talents including a gift for languages, exceptional musical skills and no small appetite for self-indulgence. Never one given to undue introspection Mort Shuman was intent on enjoying himself whenever possible – indeed, on extracting as much enjoyment as possible from every day. His home life only began to suffer when his father Louis died in 1957 and Mortie and his mother started antagonising one another. In typically brisk style (and referring to himself in the third person) Mort Shuman characterised his late adolescence as follows in his sometimes terse notes for an autobiography:

"Three things happened that were to affect Mort profoundly and they all happened about the same time. Louis died (of a heart attack, what else?), he met Doc Pomus, and he enrolled in City College."

That meeting with Doc, sandwiched by Shuman between his father's death and what was to be a short-lived spell at college although it actually came about earlier, took place because the boyfriend of a young female cousin of Doc's called Neysha introduced her to his classmate Mortie, currently in the throes of casting himself in the role of moody teenage rebel. Mort claims that after his father's death he became paranoid 'about being a momma's boy for the rest of his life' and started making life difficult for his mother Esther. "She was not allowed into the living room, which was transformed into a drinking club for young Jewish potheads," he recalled without perceptible remorse.

Mort's musical skills were remarkable and Neysha unwittingly did the world a considerable favour by guessing that, despite their age difference, Mortie and Doc might get on. Whatever the fine details, that first meeting seems to have taken place at the Brooklyn home of Morris Felder's sister Bertie (Neysha's mother) at some point in late 1954, according to Doc and Mort's independent but often hazy and conflicting recollections. Doc was scheduled to drop in and see his aunt and cousin and so Mort was invited too. There was a piano in the apartment and Mort's playing immediately told Doc that here was a talented kid with an ear for contemporary popular music that he himself seemed to lack, chiefly because he had little interest in it. Mort Shuman recalls that Doc listened to some of his solo attempts at writing what in New York was called tenement music: "You know, a redbrick building like in those Edward Hopper paintings and four or five black guys on the stoop going 'Dee-*oh*, dee *doo*, ba doo de doo de doo…' and concluded 'Yeah kid, you're OK. It's not the kind of music I *like* but…'."

He invited Mort to come and see him perform the sort of music *he* liked at a basement club, Club Musicale, in a hotel that was to become their occasional headquarters. It was no big deal. Doc liked the kid and was just doing him a favour. He even sent him along to see some friends of his called Herb Abramson, Ahmet Ertegun and Jerry Wexler who just happened to be Atlantic Records at the time. "Which was very, very funny," Mort reflected, "because Herb was a dentist, Jerry was a university professor and Ahmet and his brother Neshui were sons of the Turkish ambassador to New York. They were rhythm and blues freaks who started a record label called National in a hotel room on Broadway, and later National became Atlantic. I was sixteen or seventeen and I remember waiting outside their office shaking and a black guy came by and said, 'Don't worry about it, it's gonna be alright'. I said, 'Thank you. 'Er, by the way who are you?' He said, 'Otis. Otis Blackwell.' I went in still shaking and played and sang my first composition – 'The Curtain Fell' – and about halfway through Herb takes the high voice, Ahmet Ertegun takes the bass and they start singing with me. They gave me a $25 advance and published the song. I went back and told Doc, he was very pleased and we started writing together."

'The Curtain Fell' was recorded by The Cardinals but never released.

4

Let The Good Times Roll

The Club Musicale was the venue to which Doc invited Mort to see him perform and The Stratford Arms whose basement it occupied was one of the last of Doc's sporadic Manhattan addresses before he gravitated towards The Broadway Central around 1955. It was at the Stratford that the writing partnership began with Doc offering to give Mortie 10% (or 15% – versions differ) of every song just to sit there and watch how he worked. This arrangement puttered along for quite a while without really getting any traction. Mortie started attending City College where he ostensibly studied foreign trade during the day (when he wasn't organising the social lives of fellow students or entertaining them on piano), before working in the evening to supplement the almost non–allowance he received from home and finally joining up with Doc for a night time music education. This, according to Mortie, most usually took place in "Williamsburg, the other end of Brooklyn". Doc still lived with his parents on and off, especially when he couldn't afford even the Stratford Arms' modest rent. Then Doc experienced yet another of his sporadic strokes of luck, one which to some extent sidelined the incipient writing partnership with Mort and looked, for a while, unlikely to end in disappointment.

Doc's potential benefactor was none other than 'the father of rock'n'roll', Alan Freed, aka Moondog who'd assumed this sobriquet in 1951 when he named his R&B-only Cleveland record show *The Moondog House*. In the mid-1950s he was a DJ on New York City's WINS (1010 AM), and he latched onto Doc's recording of one of his own compositions called 'Heartlessly' on the obscure Groove label. The song was one of Doc's intermittent bids to write and perform something more radio-friendly than his staple blues repertoire and combined a love-lorn lyric with a melody punctuated by the classic blues riff that can be heard in songs as disparate as Howlin' Wolf's 'Little Red Rooster' and Peggy Lee's 'I'm A Woman' – dah-dah-dah, dah-*dah*. Freed played 'Heartlessly' daily for a week, giving it colossal exposure to a large and influential demographic. (We can only speculate whether the practice of accepting payments from record companies for airplay – known as payola – which ended Freed's career in 1959 was already in play.) In any case RCA bought the master from the local Dawn company that owned Groove, and nationwide fame seemed to be only a matter of weeks away for Doc. Then for reasons unknown RCA never released their acquisition. An educated guess would suggest that in the age of the young Elvis Presley – already a growing sensation because of his Sun recordings and to be acquired by RCA in late 1955 – the company was keenly aware that youthful good looks were now as necessary as a good voice. Sometimes good looks were *more* necessary than a good voice, a fact unkindly driven home in 1959 when Doc and Mort would be charged with writing songs so undemanding that even the handsome but vocally-challenged 26-year-old Philadelphian singer Fabiano Forte – aka Fabian – could handle them. For now the non-breakthrough of 'Heartlessly' on RCA was another crushing personal disappointment – maybe the last professional one for 30-year-old Doc who had now been hustling the clubs, promoters, managers and record companies for a dozen years.

He withdrew to his room at what was becoming his regular Manhattan home, The Broadway Central, a huge downtown sanctuary for the newly-arrived and the chronically down at heel. The eight-storey, 400-room building had declined from its original splendour as The Grand Central, "the world's largest hotel". Situated on lower Broadway between Bleecker Street and what was originally called Amity Street (now Third Street) it was already endemically sleazy by the time Doc called it home in 1955. All its clientele shared one main characteristic: they were broke. If some were young and trying to succeed in the city, most were older and in decline or hiding out from unknown threats. The lobby was redolent of theatrical careers on the skids, an atmosphere to which Doc felt he might soon become a permanent contributor. It was certainly no place to reassure a man suffering yet another setback who was already feeling that his career – such as it was – must surely be almost over. In a fitting historical footnote, the hotel, long after it had ceased to be *pied à terre* to Doc, gave up the ghost most spectacularly when one of its structural walls collapsed killing three people.

While it was still standing and in business The Broadway Central functioned as a useful enough Manhattan base for Doc and he had his own circuit of local watering holes and music joints. One day he was tipped to take in a new one, The Central Plaza Ballroom on Second Avenue where they held Friday jam sessions. Once again Doc was extraordinarily lucky, because here was to be seen another procession of famous jazzmen including several of his heroes. On his first visit it was trumpeter Roy Eldridge who had been with Gene Krupa's band and would briefly play with Artie Shaw. The audience was essentially the kind that did not impress Doc – casual jazz buffs from the better neighbourhoods plus some kids who just liked to drop in to hear Dixieland – but one of the organisers of these weekly sessions was kind enough to let Doc do his impromptu let-me-get-up-there-and-sing routine once more, and let the house band back him. This benefactor even paid him afterwards which he was certainly not expecting, and gave him an open invitation to come back and sing whenever he liked.

This unassuming man's name was Jack Crystal and if Doc took him to be a good-hearted man with little money, he was wrong. Crystal was in fact a record company executive and jazz producer who also owned and operated the famous Commodore Music Shop on West 42nd Street. Crystal always ensured Doc was paid and it was only later that Doc came to suspect that much of the money came from Crystal's own pocket. He even invited him to his home. In such ways Doc's improvised career – if indeed it was still a career – continued to lurch between disappointment, unexpected kindnesses and moments of improbable good fortune. His knack for brushing shoulders with the famous never left him. Even Jack Crystal's youngest child Billy would eventually become a celebrity, famous as a stand-up comic, movie star and serial Oscar Ceremony host.

While Doc was ploughing on with his solo singing career, Mort Shuman was also writing songs alongside his collaborative education from Doc. The song writing partnership remained informal and success remained elusive. Doc and Mort looked like an improbable team, quite unlike Doc's contemporaries Jerry Leiber and Mike Stoller who, although of conflicting temperaments were of the same age, very professional and already managing to parlay their love of R&B into songs for the teen market. This came about mainly through their songs for The Coasters, a black group with a flair for comic delivery that did not detract from their rich, tight sound. Leiber and Stoller had already written 'Hound Dog', originally recorded by Willie Mae 'Big Mama' Thornton in 1952, but it was Presley who gave it youth appeal, not the song itself. In fact Presley's 1956 remake of that song was an object lesson in how a 12-bar blues song could be reinterpreted for the youth market. Leiber and Stoller would be quick to capitalise on their good fortune not by trying to repeat the trick (impossible anyway since it had been a stroke of good fortune that made Presley pick 'Hound Dog') but by creating a distinctive youth-friendly style of song that matched a particular act. It was something Doc and Mort hoped to pull off too, but in 1956 they were still finding their way, with Doc still playing benign master to Mort's apprentice and both of them wondering how Doc's flair for the innate rhythms of blues lyrics and Mort's melodic inventiveness (as well as his playing and singing talents) might result in a hit. A superior song to the ill-fated 'Heartlessly', 'Lonely Avenue' it still identified Doc's solo song writing as being informed – and limited – by his wish to reinvent the blues for the pop market.

Robert Palmer points out in his notes to Ray Charles' *Birth Of Soul* boxed set of Ray Charles' early recordings that the inspiration for 'Lonely Avenue' seemed to have been The Pilgrim Travelers' recording of gospel song 'How Jesus Died'. 'Inspiration' might seem to be a euphemism to anyone who had heard The Pilgrim Travelers' version, which after a slow introduction launches into what sounds both melodically and rhythmically pretty much like a sketch for Doc's song. Understandably Doc never dwelt on the similarity and preferred instead to comment on his song's apparent appeal to junkies. "Mac (Mac Rebbenack, aka Dr. John) always said that was the 'junker blues' – junker being the old term for junkie," explained Doc. "It's got a monotonous and sad lyrical line that for some reason has always attracted junkies. Da-dum, da-dum, da-dum. I imagine they're shuffling along to it or something." Ray Charles gave 'Lonely Avenue' a soulful, textured treatment on a single whose B-side was Charles' own 'composition' 'Leave My Woman Alone' which borrowed even more obviously from an original gospel song, 'Leave That Liar Alone'. Charles openly acknowledged The Pilgrim Travelers' influence on his secularisation of gospel songs, particularly after they added Jesse Whitaker as a baritone in 1947. When Charles' version was covered by The Everly Brothers in 1958 'Leave That Liar Alone' had appeared as a gospel number, a soul number and a country rock number.

Albeit with a Ray Charles R&B smash hit under his belt Doc, still unlucky in love, had by now set his sights on Wilma Burke, an aspiring actress from the Midwest who was also staying at The Broadway Central where she was sharing a room with a girl called Bobby who wanted to be an artist. Doc became obsessed by blonde and beautiful Wilma, drawing her into long conversations, first in the hotel lobby then in his room. Wilma, from small-town Westville,

Illinois, was impressed with Doc's worldly-wise manner, his fund of knowledge and his colourful anecdotes about the strange sub-stratum of show business he seemed to inhabit in New York. Bobby joined their regular meetings, and occasionally so did Doc's brother Raoul who was in between careers (medicine was behind him, and the law beckoned) and his cousin Bernard who was now a cartoonist at *The New Yorker*. Under Doc's stewardship this low-rent Algonquin set talked through the nights about life, love, art, music and although ingénue Wilma from the Midwest was understandably impressed she could still see that Doc hoped to have personal relationship with her. Just before she went home for Christmas of 1956, Wilma tactfully made it clear to Doc that fond as she was of him, they were not destined to be a couple. No stranger to disappointment, he took it stoically although it was almost certainly the bitterest of blows.

Dispirited and rattling around a freezing and comparatively deserted New York, that holiday season Doc dropped in to see Ahmet Ertegun at Atlantic where he planned to let him hear a home-made demo of a couple of early Pomus/Shuman songs he hoped Atlantic would pitch to one of their signed singers. ('I Need A Girl' and 'Love Roller Coaster' would in fact be recorded by Big Joe Turner.) While waiting for Ahmet that day Doc he met Mike Stoller and Jerry Leiber at the time basking in the unexpected and belated triumph of 'Hound Dog' courtesy of Elvis Presley. Stoller had heard of Doc and Doc had heard of Leiber and Stoller's success which he envied. It seemed that their contact with publishers Hill & Range Music promised direct access to Presley. The same publishers had also furnished Presley with 'Don't Be Cruel' written by Doc's old Brooklyn pal Otis Blackwell and it was released as the other side of 'Hound Dog', vying with it for the single's place in the charts in July 1956. Doc was right to be interested in Hill & Range Music. It was to prove highly significant in making Pomus & Shuman a successful song writing team.

Formed by Julian Aberbach in Los Angeles in 1945, Hill & Range Music came to dominate country music publishing in the 1950s, publishing Spade Cooley, Lefty Frizzell, Bob Wills & His Texas

Playboys, Red Foley, Ernest Tubb, Eddy Arnold, Hank Snow and Johnny Cash among others. In a short period of time Aberbach acquired around 75% of the publishing market in Nashville, the town that called itself Music City USA. Now, incredibly, Aberbach had struck a deal that effectively meant between 1956 and the early 1970s, Elvis Presley could only record songs published by Hill & Range. In exchange for this license to print money, publishing profits were split between Presley and his management, and Hill & Range Music. Aberbach, now joined by his brother Jean, set up two Hill & Range subsidiaries, Elvis Presley Music and Gladys Music (one for each of the two rival performing rights organisations ASCAP and BMI), to stable the cash cow, putting a cousin, Freddy Bienstock, in charge. Now all they needed were songwriters to supply them with the material. Leiber and Stoller were recruited early on even though Blackwell's 'Don't Be Cruel' was the first Hill & Range song to benefit from the Presley deal. It meant Blackwell sharing writing credits with Elvis Presley who early in his career was often credited with co-authoring songs although he never actually wrote anything at all, but Blackwell, hitherto working in a tailor's shop in Brooklyn, was not going to demur. There was a buzz in the air. Doc gave Mike Stoller a song he was working on, 'Young Blood', but had been unable to finish satisfactorily. Perhaps the golden duo could do something with it and maybe their magic would rub off.

While Wilma Burke was home with her mother Lena over the Christmas holidays Doc, so recently rejected in person by his dream girl, phoned her there and proposed. Stunned, she told him she would think about it. Unknown to Doc, he was about to profit from some miraculously good timing. Things in the Westville home were looking bleak and for the first time ever Wilma, energised by her metropolitan experiences, rebelled against her strong-willed mother who was appalled by the idea of her daughter even thinking of marrying Doc whom her daughter described to her in unvarnished terms. Wilma's father Johnny Burke was not home, which perhaps was a blessing given his past history of violence towards his wife and occasionally towards Wilma too. If she was looking for a man Wilma was clearly primed to look for a benign father figure rather than the hometown high school football hero and trainee cop with whom she had split up to move to New York. Mother and daughter parted on strained terms and, anxious to assert her independence, Wilma returned to New York and promptly accepted Doc's proposal. Nineteen fifty-seven looked like being Doc's year.

★   ★   ★

In March of 1957 The Coasters had a hit with 'Young Blood'. Doc allowed that it was a barely recognisable reworking of the song he had given to Mike Stoller but he was credited as co-songwriter along with them. Legend has it that Doc first heard it playing on a roadhouse jukebox on his way back from his honeymoon and immediately called Atlantic Records from a payphone and secured an advance. Since this would have been in July of 1957, four months after the song had charted, it seems unlikely that this was the first Doc had heard about it or that, as he maintains, Jerry Wexler picked up the phone and said, "Hiya Doc. I guess you must have heard. It's a smash!"

In fact Doc's version of the song's back story anyway varied from Leiber and Stoller's who claimed that it was really only the title they inherited. Jerry Leiber said, "I was talking to Jerry Wexler one day in his office and he said, 'Look, I know you guys don't write with anyone else, but... I got a title that Doc Pomus came up with. I've talked to him for weeks, and he can't find a way to make the song happen.' I said, 'Are you sure Doc would approve of us writing it?' He said, 'Doc asked me to show it to you.' So I said, 'What's the title?' He said, 'Young Blood'. I said, 'You got it. Invite me home for dinner and I'll write it in the car.' By the time we got to his house the lyrics were 90% written." Mike Stoller says he then wrote the melody in the Atlantic studios and a hastily assembled configuration of The Coasters with a substitute singer standing in for a missing regular cut the track quickly despite cracking up at the infectiously comic effect of each of them taking a turn at the repeated phrase 'look-a-there', 'look-a-there', 'look-a-there'.

Doc Pomus sounds to have been pretty lucky to have ridden on the coattails of Leiber and Stoller *and* received a song credit and thus a share of the money. Many others would have cut him out but Leiber and Stoller were decent men. Even so, Doc always seemed to be a little aggrieved about it and in 1982 said, "Most of the articles about 'Young Blood' never mention my name. Although Leiber and Stoller wrote most of the song, the title and concept was mine." Whatever the truth about 'Young Blood' it placed Doc Pomus in the company of Leiber and Stoller who had the golden knack of writing hits for the youth market. If it had been their contribution that assured the song's success, there was still the chance that Mort, who was a quick study, could add the melodic magic to Doc's lyrics and pull off the same trick. The partnership was already starting to look promising.

In May Doc arranged a surprise for both Wilma (henceforth known as Willi to Doc and everyone else) and Mort (Bobby came along too, to make up a foursome). It was, Doc announced, a road trip a Newark blues club. The destination was hardly the surprise – Mort was driving – but the star of the show was. Big Joe Turner was appearing for one night only, and when he appeared Willi discovered that this gigantic and presumably famous blues performer was on good personal terms with her husband to be. In fact the two had started to become close at Atlantic Records when Doc pitched songs he hoped his hero would cut. He recalled, "At... first I was too poor to make demos and I would sing the songs to Ahmet Ertegun and Herb Abramson. Joe Turner couldn't read or write so I had to do a piano and voice demo for him so he could memorise the lyrics. Every once in a while I had to go to a session and whisper the lyrics in his ear. When you hear the records, you wouldn't believe that was so. He did the songs magnificently."

When Turner began to sing that night in Jersey, Mort, for his part, learned that Doc had successfully placed their co-composition

'Love Roller Coaster' with Turner who had recorded it along with 'I Need A Girl'. It was night of sweet triumph for Doc. At a stroke he had written a song for his greatest hero, impressed his fiancée and demonstrated to Mort that he, Doc, was the senior partner and that they really might have some sort of song writing career together.

There was a catered engagement party held on Long Island and much later Doc wrote movingly in his journal about his father on the drive back along Sunrise Highway. The perennially unfulfilled and irascible Morris was behind the wheel, and temporarily transformed by the unexpected celebrations, he suddenly burst into song. Millie, Doc and Willi heard his joyously unmusical rendition of 'Let The Rest Of The World Go By', a sentimental 1919 ballad of the sort Doc particularly disliked. Morris' pitch was shaky but no one could doubt his sincerity. That moment came flooding back to Doc in 1979, the year after his father's death, when he bought a Willie Nelson cassette featuring 'Let The Rest Of The World Go By'. "I played it over and over again," he wrote. "One day while playing it I suddenly and unexpectedly began to sob. I went on and on – I couldn't stop until I was raw and empty inside and almost out of tears forever."

On June 27, 1957 (his birthday), 32-year-old Jerome Felder and 24-year-old Wilma Burke were married at a Roman Catholic church, St. Joseph's, in Greenwich Village. Raoul, Bernard, Bobby, Mort and one or two other friends made up the sparse guest list for the church ceremony which was never going to be attended by Millie and Morris on religious grounds. Even so the Felders' delight that Jerome had not only found a bride but a charming and beautiful one, far outweighed any disappointment over her *shiksa* status, and for the duration of the secular marriage celebrations at least – and to everyone's amazement – their own chronic marital hostilities were suspended or at least suppressed. They even moved due south to Brooklyn's Sheepshead Bay and gave the lease of the McKibbin Street apartment to the newlyweds. Some year... and it was still only summer.

★ ★ ★

Doc's 'Young Blood' payday – not to mention his recent run of good fortune with the Big Joe Turner songs – prompted him to revive his hopes of more returns from popular song writing. Mort started to loom larger in his plans because despite Doc's senior status there was no denying that the kid, now coming up to 19, was a real talent. His singing and playing abilities were exceptional, but the variety of his melodic suggestions derived from his will-o'-the-wisp temperament and magpie inclination to garner musical cues from many sources. Like Doc he revered black music but he also loved Latin rhythms (Mort coined the word 'mambonik' to describe himself, presumably referencing the more familiar 'beatnik') as well as country music and what was not yet called World Music.

When the duo demonstrated their song ideas, Doc might take the vocal on a bluesy composition but it was Mort who had the stylistic range to tackle pop-oriented numbers. Unhappily for Doc Mort was also unpredictable, a slave to his whims as well as maintaining a multi-tasking schedule: paying lip service to his continuing City College studies, trying to earn a buck here and there, working with Doc and visiting home. Doc disapproved of Mort's unpunctuality and undependability, but it was in part an inevitable result of the age difference and the temperamental and physical mismatches between stationary Doc and spring-heeled Mort. That said, Pomus-Shuman had already turned out some promising songs. The Tibbs Brothers' '(Wake Up) Miss Rip Van Winkle' always sounded like a rather desperate novelty song although the other side, the equally jokey 'I'm Going Crazy' was more satisfying even if it was a far cry from what Andrew Tibbs aspired to. The stand-out Pomus-Shuman curio had perhaps been a song for Guitar Slim (Eddie Jones), a young black singer guitarist from Greenwood, Mississippi via Louisiana who back in 1953 had actually done what Jimi Hendrix was credited with starting a decade later: he wore outrageous costumes and played distorted electric guitar riffs overlaid on songs with recognisable blues roots. His best known number, 'Things That I Used To Do', was a minor hit in

1953 and predated Pomus-Shuman's first meeting, but circa 1956 he recorded their 'Hello, How Ya Been? Goodbye', which is still worth a listen. The Platters cut Doc and Mort's '(You've Got) The Magic Touch' in 1956 which, to its credit, sounds perfectly suited to this highly distinctive group. Again, writing about himself in the third person Mort described the period rather breathlessly in his biographical notes.

"… life became school; doing badly (except in Philosophy). Doc; writing better and better. Mom; home was hell… he wrote rock'n'roll but lived, ate, drank and breathed Latino, and mostly in an old funky ballroom on West 53rd Street and Broadway; the Palladium. … Wednesday night at the Palladium was a New York institution.

"The Mambo became important and so did Jazz. And so did the black experience. His curly hair helped. He imagined that somewhere in another life he had black ancestors. … He was still writing with Doc in Williamsburg. The lone ranger of the subway system. College was worse, but he organised great parties in the lounges and getting young singers like Dion and Bobby Darin to perform for all they could eat and drink. And he started hanging out with better known Jazz musicians: Horace Silver, Art Taylor, Johnny Griffin. And he wanted to be a great rock'n'roll writer and the white Thelonius Monk…'

Mort then started taking piano lessons with Duke Jordan up in Harlem. Jordan, who was a little older than Doc, had, along with Miles Davis, already been a regular member of Charlie Parker's quintet in the late 1940s. It was yet another creative distraction. So, complementing and occasionally annoying one another, Pomus and Shuman still shared ambition dreams of success. Instead of bachelor Doc ploughing his lonely blues furrow towards the sunset, it was now married man Doc working with a gifted if feckless young musician who was a lot closer to the age of the target rock'n'roll consumer, and hoping for a new dawn. There was a fresh neighbourhood to work too. Instead of the diffused network of blues clubs from Newark, New Jersey to Bedford-Stuyvesant, Brooklyn, there was now a very compact stamping ground for songwriters like them. These days the Broadway patch north of Times Square in Manhattan was where the song writing and publishing deals were being done.

5

Low Profile Heroes In
High Rise Offices

Success did not come at once and Doc was starting to worry about money again because now Willi was pregnant. Even the McKibbin Street neighbourhood was beginning to degenerate and seemed less safe after Willi was harassed by a street gang. It can only have been out of desperation that Doc and Mort accepted a screwball offer from a casual acquaintance to front a non-existent record company in a tiny shared office at 1650 Broadway. This unnamed building was at the corner with 51st Street on which its main entrance was located. Close to The Winter Garden Theatre it was a rather anonymous ten-storey structure to which Doc and Mort became regular visitors because it housed, among others, the offices of Hill & Range Music, the publishers to whom Otis Blackwell had sold 'Don't Be Cruel' for Elvis in 1956.

Sixteen-fifty was gradually becoming home to an assortment small of music publishers who were more interested in emergent rock'n'roll than the golden age of song writing, which was still being serviced – in a spirit of growing pessimism – by publishers in the nearby Brill

Building at 1619 Broadway. It was true that some new pop music was being published from Brill Building offices but those in the know went to 1650 Broadway first.

Meanwhile father-to-be Doc was compelled to clutch at straws. He agreed to a convoluted and decidedly dubious offer from a casual acquaintance to front a non-existent music publishing business in a tiny office at 1650 (actually half an office otherwise given over to film storage). Mort would get a token $20 a week for doing nothing while Doc would get nothing for doing nothing even though future lump sum pay offs were promised. They were simply there to provide an alibi for the man who was stringing along the elderly millionairess he had recently married and who was bankrolling this effectively non-existent publishing venture. The man was pretending to spend his time running it while actually conducting assignations elsewhere and therefore needed employees to man the phone and support his story. Doc thought any foothold in 1650 Broadway might be advantageous. He even made up a name for the imaginary company (R&B Records) and, possibly losing his grasp on reality altogether, actually signed an obscure black group – The Five Crowns – that wandered into its cramped confines on the reasonable but false assumption that an outfit called R&B Records in a building populated with song publishers might actually be in the music business. Doc dug out a Pomus-Shuman song, cut a record with them for peanuts and unexpectedly The Five Crowns subsequently had a local hit in the Pittsburgh area with 'Kiss And Make Up'. However, payment for this first hit depended on supplying a follow-up recording which no one could afford to finance. Despite this The Five Crowns liked to hang around the tiny office where there was nothing else to do other than shoot the breeze. Doc was particularly impressed with band member Benjamin Nelson whom he vaguely remembered from his own performing days.

Another visitor who occasionally sang on some of Doc and Mort's demos was Robert Walden Cassotto, aka Bobby Darin, a young man in a hurry whom Mort claimed he had once hired to sing for food and drink at one of his college concerts. Following childhood rheumatic fever Cassotto had a heart condition that did not encourage him to expect a long life, hence his haste to get on. A musical chameleon, he could sing in any style with startling facility although his ultimate ambition was to be another Frank Sinatra. Once he started to become famous he was fond of telling the press that his ambition was to be a legend in his time (country song writer Don Gibson liked Darin's phrase and wrote one of his best songs around it: '[I'd Be] A Legend In My Time'). For now though Cassotto/Darin was hit-free and hustling, afraid that Atco, his label, was about to drop him after a handful of unsuccessful releases. Nor were Pomus and Shuman doing all that well in the hit stakes. Their 1958 bid to be hip consisted of an unimaginative response to Marty Robbins' hit 'A White Sport Coat And A Pink Carnation'. Called 'White Bucks And Saddle Shoes' it was only derivative in its title and in fact had a livelier melody than Robbins' song. 'White Bucks…' was a minor hit for Bobby Pedrick Jr. (Robert John Pedrick, later to record as Robert John under which name he had a US number one hit with 'Sad Eyes' in 1979). It was also recorded in the UK by The Vernons Girls, of whom more later. For a follow up Pomus/Shuman wrote Pedrick 'Pajama Party', the sartorial theme suggesting that Doc was still looking for a formula rather than to create something original.

The R&B Records subterfuge soon collapsed, but The Five Crowns had struck lucky winning the strange honour of becoming the latest version of The Drifters, a 'brand' that was owned by Sarah Vaughan's trumpeter husband George Treadwell who simply repopulated or reinvented it from time to time as members left, singly or en masse. Benjamin Nelson, soon to be rechristened Ben E. King, would become an even more memorable member of The Drifters than the group's previously most high-profile alumnus, Clyde McPhatter, who, pre Drifters, had recorded one of Pomus and Shuman's earliest submissions to Atlantic 'My Island Of Dreams', a pretty song swamped by strings. Doc and Mort, of course, were back to square one and, to make matters simultaneously both better and worse, on May 16, 1958 Doc became the father of baby Sharon Ruth Felder.

In a timely and generous gesture Otis Blackwell introduced Doc and Mort to the influential Paul Case of Hill & Range in the hope of boosting their pitching chances on the eighth floor of 1650 Broadway. Case was the man with his finger on the pulse of rock'n'roll. Long in the music business he had the touch that neither the Aberbach brothers nor Freddie Bienstock possessed. The Viennese expatriate Aberbachs were cultured men with as little interest in rock'n'roll as they had in the country music that made their initial fortune. Businessmen whose office sported a modern art collection, their pragmatic motto when striking business deals such as the Presley arrangement was 'better 50% of something than 100% of nothing'. Case, on the other hand, knew music and songwriters and was possessed of a generous spirit. Despite their somewhat threadbare portfolio of would-be hit songs, Doc and Mort (who were now occasionally including Willi in the writing process) appealed to Case. He bought a few songs that showed no sign of breaking the pattern but then offered them what Doc really needed: a regular pay cheque. He proposed a three-year deal with another Hill & Range subsidiary, Rumbalero Music, with Doc getting $200 a week and Mort getting $100. Mort got the good news downtown during a snowstorm. Thrown out of City College because of his tendency to spend more time on piano music than studies, he was now doing manual work, unloading ships in New York Harbour in sub-zero temperatures and not eating nearly enough. Mort's third-person recollection of salvation ran like this:

"Walked about 5 miles in a snow storm to meet Doc and Elvis Presley's publisher. The man took one look at Mort and gave him $10 to go and get a meal and when he came back Mort signed an exclusive songwriters' contract with the Aberbach Brothers and Freddy Bienstock."

At this point in the story it is worth dwelling for a moment on the extraordinary career of Freddie Bienstock whose appointment by his cousins as handler of the hugely significant Presley publishing arrangement some saw as nothing more than an unremarkable act of nepotism. Bienstock was born in Switzerland in 1923 but his parents moved to Vienna when he was three. In 1938 he was sent to visit an uncle in US, but war broke out and he stayed. With a cousin in New York who had a job as a song -plugger at Chappell he eventually got a job in the company's stockroom in the early 1940s, gradually working his way up to song-plugger, a job that involved offering sheet music of new songs to prospective performers. That was his preparation for joining his cousins' company. When the Elvis gravy train eventually started to slow down Bienstock bought Hill & Range's UK subsidiary which was the basis for more shrewd deals, culminating in his acquisition of Chappell Music from PolyGram in 1984. He had risen from Chappell's storeroom clerk to its primary shareholder and president. "I got great satisfaction when I bought Chappell," was his usual quietly understated line about his amazing rise.

Back in 1958 Doc and Mort's first task for Rumbalero was the Fabian assignment which involved stripping down rejected songs originally intended for Elvis to get them within the pop idol's limited vocal range. 'I'm A Man' and 'Turn Me Loose' did the job they were intended to do, and Pomus and Shuman, hit makers, were on their way.

Arriving three days after baby Sharon, Bobby Darin's last throw of the dice for Atlantic's Atco label, 'Splish Splash', made its debut in the charts on May 19, 1958. Written by Darin and a pseudonymised disc jockey (Murray The K who, with the spectre of payola looming large, hid behind his wife's name), it was a novelty number covered in the UK by squeaky-voiced 1950s TV comedian Charlie Drake. Darin now needed more material and recorded two self-penned songs ('Early In The Morning' and 'Queen Of The Hop') before having a modest hit with Pomus and Shuman's 'Plain Jane'. They also offered him a song with a title inspired by the name of Doc's new daughter, 'I Ain't Sharin' Sharon' but Atco sat on it for a year and so Darin's recording was pre-empted by Jimmy Darren and Buddy

Knox's versions of the song. When Darin's self-penned 'Dream Lover' became a huge hit it kick-started a career which was to progress at some speed through various abrupt phases, first dipping into Brecht & Weill's *Die Dreigroschenoper* (*The Threepenny Opera*) for 'Mack The Knife', then the songbook of French singer-songwriter Charles Trenet for 'Beyond The Sea', then country, folk and a lot more besides. Always moving faster than his fans, Darin once memorably headlined a touring rock'n'roll package show in the UK in which he unsuccessfully tried to entertain rock fans still high from a thunderous set from second-billed Duane Eddy, with a slow jazzy version of 'My Funny Valentine' while sitting on the edge of the stage and loosening his tie like a world-weary Sinatra. He was 24 at the time.

Back at Rumbalero, Pomus and Shuman were starting to look like a useful investment after all. They could write to order, something Doc would always make a point of explaining to the press in case they thought he actually *liked* this sappy teen stuff. It sounded patronising and it was, even though Doc thought he was just being honest.

In truth he had spent 16 or so years failing to make a living from the blues he loved because not enough other people loved it. Millions, it seemed, loved rock'n'roll but that was a poor reason to demean it. Frank Sinatra was more outspoken. He had a traditional music publishing company in the Brill Building and did nothing to disguise his hatred of the rock'n'roll that was making him sound old fashioned. In 1957 Sinatra's ABC TV series flopped and Elvis had five times as many hits in the Top Ten as he did. Writers contributing to Presley's chart tally, including Jerry Leiber and Mike Stoller, were dubbed 'cretinous goons' by Sinatra who never behaved more like the Hoboken hoodlum he used to be than when he wasn't getting his own way. Billy Rose (William Samuel Rosenberg), impresario and lyricist, was another songwriter locked into the past and he said of Elvis Presley, "Not only are most of his songs junk, but in many cases they are obscene junk, pretty much on a level with dirty comic magazines. It's this current climate that makes Elvis Presley and his animal posturings possible."

It was Bobby Darin who introduced Doc and Mort to his friend Don Kirshner, a man who wanted to get into the business side of music. No musician himself, Kirshner was a bright, ambitious guy but no one wanted to back him until he met one Al Nevins, an older man with considerable experience in the music business. Together Al and Don formed Aldon Music and set up a modest office on the sixth floor of 1650 Broadway, two floors below Hill & Range. Contrary to all expectations Aldon Music was destined to be a huge success. Its rise began when Mort Shuman bumped into fellow alumni from Abraham Lincoln High, Neil Sedaka and Howard Greenfield. They too were having trouble pitching songs to Hill & Range so Doc and Mort suggested trying Aldon Music who were just setting up and should be a softer sell. Aldon signed Sedaka & Greenfield and soon they started having hits with Connie Francis (born Concetta Rosa Maria Franconero in the Italian quarter of Newark, New Jersey) effectively propelling her to stardom. It started with a catchy lightweight novelty number called 'Stupid Cupid'.

Meanwhile Doc and Mort were exploiting their knack for finding the right words and music for a series of young good-looking Italian-American male singers in the Fabian mould, albeit for the main part less limited vocalists. These included Bobby Rydell (Robert Ridarelli), Jimmy Darren (James Ercolani) and Frankie Avalon (Francis Avallone). Each of them had a Pomus-Shuman hit in the second half of 1959. So too did a Bronx kid by the name of Dion DiMucci who, as lead singer of Dion & The Belmonts, was given Doc and Mort's 'Teenager In Love' and became a star. The song had started life as a chirpy celebration of youth and love, and pop music historians can still hear how very cheesily it came out on Mort's early bouncy piano and vocal demo (sample lyric: 'It may be raining but the sun will be shining in my heart'). Sanity prevailed, Doc wrote new, more melancholy lyrics and Mort adjusted the melody to produce a self-pitying four-chord teen ballad. The original intention had been to write the song for a Laurie Records signing called The Mystics (yet another Brooklyn outfit) comprising Phil and Albee Cracolici,

George Galfo, Bob Ferrante and Al Contrera. The quintet had a pleasant, chiming harmony style and its members were thrilled with the final version of the song. Then politics intervened and Laurie Records – owned by Robert and Gene Schwartz and financed by Alan I. Sussel – decided the song was too good to give to The Mystics and gave it instead to labelmates Dion & The Belmonts. Lead singer Dion DiMucci recalls: "I'd just recruited a group from my neighbourhood and we called them The Belmonts. We'd come off a hit called 'I Wonder Why' and the company – hah! the company! The Schwartz Brothers – loved this record by Ricky Nelson 'Poor Little Fool', so they commissioned Doc Pomus and Mort Shuman to write 'Teenager In Love'. I remember Mort Shuman playing the song and I'm thinking Oh God, where do these people think we're at? I was looking to be cool and it was right out of my backyard, so wimpy... but The Belmonts started doing this ooh-wah thing and I just knew right away it had such a sound, I started skipping over those ooh-wahs...."

Pomus and Shuman were asked to come up with something else for The Mystics. The result was 'Hushabye', a rather routine song that nonetheless became a smash hit in May 1959, eventually spending nine weeks on the national charts, partly perhaps because Alan Freed adopted it as a suitably nocturnal sign-off theme for his Saturday Big Beat Show. Even so, Dion DiMucci got the better deal despite those initial feelings of discomfort with the love-struck lyrics he thought were inappropriate to his self-image. He respected Doc and idolised Mort – 'an amazingly talented guy' – so it was no hard sell.

Dion's keening lead vocal performance of 'Teenager In Love' was just right and everyone knew they were in on the birth of a big hit. By November 1959 it entered the Billboard Top 5. It was a hit in the UK too where three versions of the song (Dion, Marty Wilde and Craig Douglas) all entered the Top 30 while two more somewhat ill-judged cover versions, by Rikki Henderson and Dickie Valentine, did less well. Henderson was a dance band singer who regularly recorded for the UK budget cover label Embassy, sold exclusively in Woolworth stores, and Valentine was a 30-year-old vocalist firmly rooted in British light entertainment. Even so, four UK cover versions plus the original all on the market at the same time seemed to be something of an endorsement for the song. Paul Case's belief in Doc and Mort had certainly paid off and they knew that, at last, they had arrived. Their figurative arrival, however, was soon to be followed by a literal departure, the result of a transatlantic trip that would come entirely out of the blue.

At the time song writers in general were largely unknown in the United States. There was little popular interest in who they were or what they looked like. The public wanted to hear their songs and see the artists who sang them, but the writers – with the exceptions of people like Cole Porter, Rodgers & Hammerstein, George Gershwin and Jerome Kern – usually remained anonymous technicians. If you lumped together the entire songwriters working for the publishers in The Brill Building and 1016 Broadway in the late 1950s, hardly any of their names would have been recognised by the American public. Not the case, it seemed, on a small island four-and-a half thousand miles to the east of New York. If an Englishman called Jack Good was to be believed (and those who already knew this master of sleight of hand might have smiled wryly at that proviso) Britain's youth was crazy about the legendary song writing team of Doc Pomus and Mort Shuman. The duo should lose no time in accepting his invitation to visit the UK where a grateful nation would welcome them and an entire edition of Jack Good's national teen TV music show *Boy Meets Girls* would be devoted to their songs. Doc was appalled. That Roosevelt spa at Warm Springs, Georgia was the furthest from home he had ever travelled. Mort, by contrast, was as always up for a new experience, especially if it involved travel. The Aberbachs felt it was a commercially valuable offer that should not be refused.

★ ★ ★

Jack Good was an unlikely but extraordinary champion of rock'n'roll. Born in 1931 in Greenford, in West London, he went to Oxford University and might be said to be one of the first intellectuals to be a true fan of the music rather than another of the sterile academic observers whose primary interest was to draw sociological or political morals from its sudden eruption in Britain. Not that Good had ever been much tempted to withdraw to an ivory tower. He had studied at the London Academy of Music & Drama and had been president of Oxford University Dramatic Society. Drawn to acting he had some small parts in London's West End theatres, as well as teaming with writer-performer-lyricist Trevor Peacock as a comedy duo appearing at London's Windmill Theatre which had a long history of nude shows punctuated by comedy acts. There was no stopping Good who breezed into a job as a light entertainment producer at BBC Television where he was instructed, he recalled, to make a programme for adolescents: 'something with mountain climbing for boys, fashion for girls, that sort of thing'. Good simply ignored the brief and launched *6.5 Special* in 1957, a music programme for adolescents who had better things to do with their leisure time than climb mountains or follow fashion. British rocker Tommy Steele was featured as was skiffle star Lonnie Donegan and despite the slightly more 'respectable' inclusion of some jazz acts the BBC remained disapproving, insisting on a more varied magazine format.

Good promptly left and went to work for the opposition, ITV, Britain's sole commercial TV channel at the time. There he launched *Oh Boy!* in June of 1958. Broadcast live from the Hackney Empire, a venerable music hall in East London, the show became British Television's first showcase for home-grown rock'n'rollers. It helped launch the careers of young Cliff Richard, Marty Wilde and Billy Fury, all of whom were shaped by Good who saw himself as a Svengali dedicated to presenting what were Britain's three best rock'n'roll singers in the best light. Marty Wilde (born Reginald Smith) was the best and needed little help from Good or anybody else; Billy Fury (Ron Wycherly) was the moodiest looking and a fine singer to boot although Good encouraged him to look even moodier; and Cliff Richard (Harry Webb) had the dark good looks that made him the most suited to being the English Elvis and Good strove to make him look more smouldering than wholesome by getting him to curl his lip and, in performance, suddenly clutching his arm in a gesture that might have made an older performer look as if he was suffering an incipient heart attack.

Good followed *Oh Boy!* with *Boy Meets Girls* (ITV, 1959-60), now featuring Marty Wilde as presenter and performer, and the hard-working British female backing group The Vernons Girls, in attendance. (The Vernons Girls, an ever-changing ensemble, appeared as session singers on many records in the 1950s and 1960s, including Jimi Hendrix's 'Hey Joe'. As already mentioned, they recorded the Pomus Shuman song 'White Bucks And Saddle Shoes' under their own name 1958). This show also introduced genuine American rockers Eddie Cochran, Conway Twitty, Brenda Lee and Gene Vincent to the British viewing public. Good had a ball with polite Southern drawler Vincent who suffered from a limp due to a motorcycle accident sustained in the US navy but whom Good dramatised wildly by dressing him in black leather and encouraging him to adopt a Richard III persona, and lurch about the stage clutching a microphone stand – a ruined monarch from Norfolk, Virginia.

It was the *Boy Meets Girls* format that Doc and Mort were invited to grace. Good, with typical bravado, set about creating the sort of welcome consistent with the hyperbolic build-up he had promised (rarely a liar, Good, by force of enthusiasm and energy, would simply make happen what he had already told people was the case). He succeeded, laying on an airport welcoming jamboree that had Doc and Mort looking behind them to see who the disembarking celebrity might be who was inciting all this press and public excitement. Two low-profile song writers who plied their trade in a tiny office in a tall anonymous building, they were entirely unprepared to be fêted abroad, yet Good, who had shamelessly staged the welcoming committee, also arranged nights on the town with showbiz celebrities of the day, including songwriter Lionel Bart, early rocker Tommy Steele and actor/singer Anthony Newley. Most, including Jack Good, had allegiances to the British Decca record company and it seems likely that Good had simply been nominated as facilitator by Decca (after overtures from the Aberbachs) to help Doc and Mort pitch songs to British acts.

This they did, approaching London-based Italian rocker Little Tony (born Antonio Ciacchi) whom Jack Good obviously hoped would be a UK-based equivalent of all those handsome American-Italian singers like Dion. It never happened despite Little Tony taking Pomus and Shuman's 'Too Good' and 'Foxy Little Mama' for a single that peaked at number 19 in the 1960 charts. Ace guitarist Joe Brown and Marty Wilde would also record their songs. Willi and Sharon happily played mom and child tourists while Doc and Mort were taking care of business. Then, as promised, the episode of *Boy Meets Girls* aired featuring only Pomus-Shuman songs. Mort even got to perform 'I'm A Man' on it. Good then got him to record the song at the Decca studios accompanying himself on piano and with Joe Brown on guitar. He also recorded 'Turn Me Loose' for the flip side, but despite Good's enthusiasm, the record was not something Mort admired when he heard it in later years. Adam Faith, who would cross paths with Mort again in 1987 under rather different circumstances, also recorded 'I'm A Man' in 1960, with John Barry providing a dramatic backing for what was always an underpowered song.

Mort's Decca session also enabled him to lay down a voice and piano demo of a song Doc and he had written back in the States but not yet placed. He had also brought on the trip a completed song with a view to trying to get it to Elvis who was currently stationed in Germany doing military service. That song, 'It's Been Nice', he gave instead to Marty Wilde who was a thoughtful and knowledgeable music fan as well as an excellent singer and a man with whom Mort struck up an instant friendship. Almost instantly it appeared as the B-side to Wilde's 'Bad Boy' and became a favourite among Wilde's British fans, still featuring in his live performances well into the 21st century and re-recorded by him for a greatest hits compilation. Quirky, witty and memorable, its staccato rhythms and wry lyric about a girl trying to end a date gracefully without further commitment made it a stand-out Pomus-Shuman song from that era.

Joe Brown, solo performer and Decca session guitarist, was another Jack Good regular, but he was less lucky with his Pomus and Shuman songs. 'People Gotta Talk' and 'Comes The Day' were pleasant enough but did not really suit the singer who tried some ill-judged Elvis-style vocal inflections in the latter.

What the London trip also achieved was an unlikely meeting between Mort Shuman and Lamar Fike, a buddy of Elvis Presley's who was sharing a flat with him in Germany. Fike happened to be in London and for unclear reasons Mort and Lamar ("a good guy" reported Mort) even made an excursion to Manchester together 'to hang out'. No one remembers quite why, although Freddy Bienstock liked to tell a story that it was to see a show (although he misremembered the location as Birmingham) "and Lamar became like a valet to him. It was cold and Mort wanted Lamar's scarf. There was a big argument and Lamar said, 'Well take the scarf and shove it up your ass, I'm leaving'. He didn't mind doing things for Elvis but he certainly wasn't going to be a valet for Mort Shuman." One would have thought that Lamar, a big, fat good ol' boy, would have made an unlikely Jeeves (though no more unlikely that Mort's Wooster), but the spat must have been temporary because Mort always recalled their excursion with fond amusement. "Lamar Fike from Memphis and Mort Shuman from Brooklyn hanging out in Manchester at the start of the swinging sixties – that was something!" Something else was the demo that Fike promised to give to Elvis. The song was 'Mess Of Blues', arguably one of Pomus and Shuman's best compositions and, in due course, one of Elvis' greatest records.

Even though in later years Mort's memory (usually incisive for detail but hazy about context) suggested that the trip was really instigated by the Aberbachs, Jack Good's machinations on Pomus and Shuman's behalf had many consequences, most of them benign. Mort made new friends in London, a city he would return to and work in frequently and, finally, live in, and even Doc wanted to stay on but was urged to return by Willi who had already taken Sharon back home.

Mort recalled: "I was seventeen or eighteen at the time and when I got to London it was really a lot of fun. In New York I made my own fun because New York wasn't really a rock'n'roll fun town, strange as it may seem. It was a business kind of thing. You had your publishers and your record people but the artists just came in and out of town. They were really hanging out in Nashville, they were hanging out in Memphis, they were starting to hang out in L.A. So I come to London and all the stars were here having a great time."

The chance meeting with Lamar Fike (in later years Mort seemed unsure whether this happened at the tail end of that first trip or on his second visit made soon afterwards) would indeed catch Elvis' attention, and, yes, it seemed that Britain had after all warmed to the two songwriters who arrived looking like puzzled businessmen clutching portfolios but whose contribution to rock'n'roll made them welcome guests. For his part Jack Good, an outwardly jolly but uncompromising man, would continue to outrage and surprise. In the US he transferred his TV show format to create *Shindig!* in 1964, again walking out when he disagreed with the men in suits. For stage and screen he produced *Catch My Soul*, a rock musical based on *Othello*, a play which had intrigued him since his youthful days on the London stage. He popped up in everything from TV specials and an Elvis film (*Clambake*) to a Cary Grant WW2 comedy called *Father Goose* where his brief cameo as a servile naval man trying to ingratiate himself with Trevor Howard's superior officer is a miniature delight that suggests Good could have made a career as an accomplished character actor had he so chosen. With such a colourful history it should come as no surprise that in his later years Good converted to Catholicism and became a hermit-like artist, based first in New

Mexico and then back in Britain in Oxfordshire, dedicating himself to painting icons.

Back home in New York Doc and Mort discovered that in their absence Hill & Range had relocated to the penthouse of The Brill Building. Ten Pomus-Shuman hits in 1959 put them only two short of the 12 achieved by the undisputed masters Leiber and Stoller in that year. These and the advantageous Elvis Presley Music deal had rocket-boosted Hill & Range's success putting them literally at the very top of The Brill Building, stoking Sinatra's now near-pathological hatred of rock'n'roll and hardly endearing them to the less volatile publishing advocates of MOR popular music.

Pomus and Shuman started work again, once again low profile heroes but now at the top of a taller building, albeit (at their own request) in a scruffy little windowless office where they felt more at home rather than in the luxurious quarters with a commanding view that Jean Aberbach offered them. Experience had conditioned them to work best in cramped rooms, and Mort in particular needed no extra distractions to divert him from the task in hand. No longer the junior apprentice he was now a fully-fledged partner and, arguably, with his multiple musical skills, already the primary driver of the Pomus-Shuman hit machine. Mort was making good money that he would lose no time converting into hedonistic pleasures. Doc, the family man, would use his to move out of the city and buy a home in Lynbrook, Long Island.

6

Brill Building Days

The Brill Building at 1619 Broadway has become something of a false icon in the history of popular music. If its fame is misleading it is also understandable. Unlike its influential Broadway counterpart 1650, it actually had a name (originally the Lefcourt Building after its developer, latterly The Brill Building after its street-level haberdasher tenants). It also had The Turf Restaurant on one side Jack Dempsey's restaurant on the other; after a while it also acquired an elaborately fretted golden Art Deco entrance, and (from the 1970s to 2012) a relocated music store on its corner with West 49th. Colony was a music retailer that became part of Broadway's history. In truth the new Tin Pan Alley spilled over into many other nearby buildings too, not just 1650, but The Brill, which had enjoyed the cachet of housing famous song publishers for longer than most, became handy shorthand for a remarkable explosion of New York-based, almost exclusively Jewish song writing talent that was to dominate the landscape of pop music from the late 1950s to pre-Beatles 1960s.

Not all of the popularly assumed Brill Building song writers even started there. Neil Sedaka & Howard Greenfield, Carole King & Gerry Goffin, and Cynthia Weil & Barry Mann all plied their trade

61

for Aldon Music in the 1650 Broadway building to begin with and so did a number of less well-known writers. Founders Don Kirshner and Al Nevins subscribed to the prevailing view that the new pop music could retool the music business based on models of previous decades, spot new talent and retain control of the whole process. Kirshner railed at the two-cent mechanical royalties his company received for each record sold so he and Nevins became independent producers supplying the finished masters to the recording labels. Now Aldon was able to place its songs on both sides of a record so doubling the mechanical income, as well as getting a royalty on each record sold. Eventually Aldon could demand a 10% royalty, with half going to the artist and half going to the company. In the process it became a tight-knit, at times professionally incestuous outfit; Howard Greenfield wrote with Jack Keller when Neil Sedaka was unavailable and once Keller and Greenfield swapped writing partners with Gerry Goffin and Carole King for a joke. Goffin and Keller came up with a song that eventually did nothing for the career of Jack Jones while King and Greenfield wrote the sublime 'Crying In The Rain' which gave The Everly Brothers their last big hit. Kirshner liked to encourage competition and collaboration in his business which was now occupying most of the top floor of 1650. In the same playful spirit Carole King once even borrowed Mort Shuman's name for a jokey 'answer' record to a hit by Annette Funicello called 'Tall Paul'. King's uncharacteristic rocker 'Short Mort' ('In his elevator shoes/with a nine-inch sole/he still looks like/he's standing in a hole') could hardly have given offence since from adolescence Mort Shuman towered over most people he met, including Carole King.

Up in The Brill Building, Hill & Range were about to see Pomus and Shuman enter their golden period almost as soon as they got back from Britain. Before Doc and Mort went on their transatlantic adventure the latest holders of The Drifters moniker – the former Five Crowns – had enjoyed some success with a record whose Pomus-Shuman A-side, '(If You Cry) True Love, True Love' (lead singer

Johnny Lee Williams) was outperformed by its nominal B-side, a Ben E. King composition on which he sang lead, 'There Goes My Baby'. As live performers, the new Drifters were not doing well on circuits where no one could fail to notice the latest complete change of personnel sometimes struggling with what was supposed to be their own back catalogue. However their 'owner' Treadwell maintained good relations with Atlantic Records who still rated Leiber and Stoller highly as record producers and who accordingly had produced this first hit for the new group. As writers Leiber and Stoller's Coasters' sharply-observed songs often poked affectionate fun at the preoccupations and mannerisms of young blacks, but they knew this would not suit The Drifters. They looked instead to find songs to match the more romantic mood projected by this group with the charismatic lead singer. Mike and Jerry, who had already introduced a more textured sound to 'There Goes My Baby' and '(If You Cry) True Love, True Love' again approached Doc and Mort who responded at first efficiently and then magnificently. Everything seemed to be coming together. At the time Doc thought Jerry Leiber and Mike Stoller were geniuses for parlaying their love of black music into the sort of success he never could. In turn Jerry and Mike had great respect for Doc and although the much younger and more flighty Mort never really entered their social circle they saw his talent and drew on his feverish enthusiasm for Latin music. Like Mort, Mike Stoller had been a 'mambonik' when a teenager and so the increasingly dense orchestral backings Leiber and Stoller were playing with started to take on a more Latin flavour.

At this point it seems worth pausing to contextualise the impact of Hispanic forms on the musical landscape of New York in the late 1950s. At street level it was simply a gut-feeling response fostered by a growing Hispanic population and the neighbourhoods they inhabited. Where The Lincoln Center now stands was once the province of the racially tense working class district fictionalised in the 1957 Broadway musical *West Side Story*. The show's reworking of the Romeo & Juliet plot had started life in 1949 by recasting the Montagus and Capulets as Jewish and Irish gangs, but after a number of false starts Arthur Laurents (né Levine), who eventually wrote the book, Stephen Sondheim, who wrote the lyrics, and composer Leonard Bernstein settled on a central conflict between Polish-American and Puerto Rican immigrant gangs. The setting was that now-gentrified Upper West Side district of the West 50s and 60s and the musical was rich with Hispanic-flavoured musical themes. Admittedly it was a stylisation but it was a good one and *West Side Story* became world-famous first through the show and then all over again four years later because of the film. The show's Broadway debut on September 26, 1957, was at the Winter Garden Theatre whose address, 1634 Broadway, placed it in close proximity to both The Brill Building and number 1650.

Mort Shuman, of course, had already steeped himself in the real thing at the Palladium at West 53rd Street and Broadway. "Stars of stage and screen danced and drank with cleaning ladies, seamstresses, pimps, pushers," he wrote, "and MS was in the middle, not only on Wednesday night but Friday, Saturday and Sunday too. And there fell in with the inter-racial crowd, the outcasts – not wanted by either side." He continued his third-person recollection: "The Mambo became important and so did Jazz. And so did the black experience. His curly hair helped. He imagined that somewhere in another life he had black ancestors. He started hanging out with second-rate Latin and Jazz musicians and Mambo dancers. All black. Walk black and eat black. Because as everyone knew, black was "soul" and white, Jewish, lower middle-class America had none."

Norman Mailer, in his 1957 'White Negro' essay had expressed parallel sentiments: "In such places as Greenwich Village a *menage-a-trois* was completed – the bohemian and the juvenile delinquent came face-to-face with the Negro, and the hipster was a fact in American life....

"The Negro has the simplest of alternatives: live a life of constant humility or ever-threatening danger... and in his music he gave voice to the character and quality of his existence, to his rage and the infinite variations of joy, lust, languor, growl, cramp, pinch, scream and despair of his orgasm. For jazz is orgasm, it is the music of orgasm… it spoke… of instantaneous existential states to which some whites could respond, it was indeed a communication by art because it said, 'I feel this, and now you do too.'"

Although the interplay of Latin rhythms, black soul and outsider Jewish musical sensibilities may look like an odd mix or even a phoney one when seen one out of context, it was the legitimate result of demographic forces at play in New York in the late 1950s. The city's Puerto Rican population had more than doubled in the 1940s, reaching well over 600,000. New York itself had always been a racial melting pot and the drift of its neighbourhoods in the late 1950s and early 1960s as well as the vagaries of city planning had simply made cultural interaction inevitable. Even the tamest of the budding young Jewish pop songwriters, Neil Sedaka, claimed the cha cha as a major influence alongside Tchaikovsky and Stravinsky in his Abraham Lincoln High year book, and later he claimed Latin music had hit New York like a craze at the same time as rock'n'roll.

All of which helps to explain why The Drifters, a black group, were to succeed with a clutch of variously Latin-flavoured songs often written by the Jewish team of Pomus and Shuman and produced by another Jewish team, Leiber and Stoller. 'This Magic Moment' was a triumph, a flowing romantic Shuman melody complete with Spanish guitar, while 'Room Full Of Tears' begins almost like a flamenco number. Nothing can quite explain how the sublime 'Save The Last Dance For Me' came about even though there are plenty of theories. Was the song Doc and Mort wrote and the sound Leiber and Stoller achieved influenced by Mort Shuman's recent trip to Mexico, part of his wild celebrations as a result of the success of 'This Magic Moment', proof that he had arrived and that heavy duty partying was called for? (In Mort's world 'wine, women and song' was not a cliché, it was an agenda.) Was the song animated by the passion of Doc's title originally scribbled on the back of an invitation at his own wedding celebrations when, for obvious reasons, he could not dance with his new wife but was pleased for others to do so... as long as it was clear who would be taking her home? (It seems likely that he jotted down the title and a few lines and then put it to one side until needed.) Brilliant as Doc's finished lyric is, it is Shuman's soaring, flowing melody with its syncopated and contrasting Latin bridge that makes the song truly memorable. Several commentators have mentioned how some of the lyrics add to the exotic flavour of the song by sounding like a careful translation from a foreign language. It is true. 'Don't forget who's taking you home and in whose arms you're gonna be' may not sound like a vernacular American English pop lyric but it is elegant and grammatical writing... one might even dare say that it anticipates the lyrics of Björn Ulvaeus, a Swede whose meticulous attempts to write English lyrics for Abba sometimes produced similarly straitened locutions, grammatically exact, but arrestingly unexpected because of their formal correctness. ('There's not, I think, a single episode of *Dallas* that I didn't see' is a case in point from Abba's final haunting single, 'The Day Before You Came'.) Weirdly, 'Save The Last Dance for Me' was deemed by the record company to be a B-side. The A-side was supposed to be a fairly routine Pomus and Shuman song with little more than cascading strings and a catchy melody to recommend it, 'Nobody But Me'. Not for the first time the DJs redressed the imbalance.

However, 1960 was not all about The Drifters and Latin music. Pomus and Shuman were turning out a lot of material, much of it good, some of it indifferent and one or two songs that are hard to admire. One of the weirdest was surely 'Desdemona's Lament', a scat song recorded by one of Duke Ellington's favourite vocalists, Joya Sherrill. The explanation for this strange jazzy departure seems to be that it was intended for a film – *Visit To A Small Planet* – based on a book by Gore Vidal and starring Jerry Lewis, the mid-20th century comedian who makes Jim Carrey look restrained by comparison. Then, in early July, Elvis' sensational recording of Pomus and

66

Shuman's 'A Mess Of Blues' was released in the US as the B-side of 'It's Now Or Never'. The A-side was a pretentious mock-operatic version of 'O Sole Mio', a Neapolitan song written at the end of the 19th century and already sung by Enrico Caruso, Beniamino Gigli and Mario Lanza. 'It's Now Or Never' sported English lyrics by Aaron Schroeder and Wally Gold and It got to number one while its flipside 'Mess Of Blues' reached number 32 in its own right. Doc and Mort's immediate reward was a thankless task: supply a new English lyric to another piece of Italian cheese, this time 'Torna a Surriento', another Neapolitan classic only a few years younger than 'O Sole Mio'. It already had English lyrics but new ones were deemed necessary for Presley. Mort handed the thankless lyric-only task over to Doc who did a professional job and rechristened it 'Surrender' (a neat English echo of the Sorrento of the original) while Mort's only contribution was to demo it and throw in a single musical embellishment. Mort recalled: "There's a point in the demo of 'Surrender' where it breaks and we went from minor to major with the singing: 'Won't you please surrender to me?' Elvis did that exactly the way I did it, which made me feel good. It was nice to feel he was really listening to those demos."

'A Mess Of Blues' (a phrase of Doc's which Presley sang as 'A mess of the blues') was released as an A-side in other territories and, as part of Elvis' first single following his discharge from the army, it reassured some fans that he was still in touch with the bluesy strand of his electrifying early recordings. Pseudo-operatic re-treads like 'It's Now Or Never' sent out a less encouraging message that Elvis was about to go down the dreaded all-round-entertainer route.

'I Count The Tears' was the last Pomus-Shuman/Drifters hit of 1960 and it was one of their strongest songs, subsequently recorded by Irma Thomas, Rosanne Cash, Gerry & The Pacemakers, The Dakotas, Lloyd Price and many more. The single marked the last official appearance of Ben E. King as lead singer. He left intending to give up the business altogether but was persuaded to pursue a solo career.

Nineteen sixty-one would prove a prolific year for Doc and Mort, with 13 of their songs charting – more than one a month. They had made it. Still trying was Cynthia Weil who, with Barry Mann, would become a highly successful songwriter. All her life she recalled Mort giving her encouragement in the reception area of Hill & Range. "I was a rank Beginner, clutching my demo nervously, waiting to play it for the professional manager and Mort was lounging in a corner, reading a magazine, a guy oozing confidence, a writer with hits under his belt, someone who obviously knew the game.

"He introduced himself and we started to talk and he calmed me down, made me laugh, filled me in on what I needed to know and gave me a pep talk so that I almost felt a little confidence rubbing off on me. It meant so much to a novice to have that kind of attention from a pro. He wished me luck and I actually got my first advance that day, $50."

In 1961 'Señor Big And Fine' was recorded by LaVern Baker, a Chicago-born black singer who recorded for Atlantic from 1953 to 1954 and enjoyed her biggest success with 'Jim Dandy' in 1956. 'Señor Big And Fine' was a near-novelty Pomus-Shuman song whose Hispanic influence owed little to the instrumentation or arrangement. It appeared only on Baker's album *Saved* but in 1961 she would also record an 'answer' record to one of Pomus and Shuman's biggest successes of the year.

'A Texan And A Girl From Mexico' was obviously a bid to create a Connie Francis-type hit, in this case for Anita Bryant, an ex-beauty pageant winner later to become notorious in the US for her right-wing, anti-gay campaigning. The record only struggled to number 85 in the pop charts despite a good melody, its well-tried 'lovers-separated-by-culture' theme, and Bryant's incisively double-tracked harmony vocals à la Francis.

To complete this clutch of overtly South of the Border songs, also in 1961 when Ben E. King had become a solo act with his own towering song 'Stand By Me' (co-written with Leiber and Stoller) under his belt, he remembered Doc and Mort and recorded their 'Souvenir Of Mexico'. His recording also revisited the Latin sound of his Drifters' cuts and possibly saw him collaborating in a risqué double entendre since the phrase had a vernacular connotation to do with sexually transmitted diseases.

Pomus and Shuman's 1961 song 'Sweets For My Sweet' is overtly influenced by Afro-Cuban music, at least in The Drifters' version. Even the more colourless but very successful British cover version by The Searchers cannot disguise a distinctive and repetitive chord progression redolent of 'La Bamba', the classic Mexican folk song in the *Son Jarocho* style that combines Spanish and African musical elements. Mexican-American singer Ritchie Valens (Richard Valenzuela) had made 'La Bamba' an American hit in 1958, the year before he died and three years before The Drifters had this hit. Mort Shuman felt that The Searchers' version was not necessarily inferior to The Drifters', just different. "It was a different sort of sound," he replied when asked about it on Merseyside radio by Spencer Leigh, "and of course they didn't have me playing on the piano as The Drifters did (!) but I also think there was so much enthusiasm so even if perhaps technically or musically it was not really the greatest, it was so infectious."

The Drifters' lead singer was now Charlie Thomas although Ben E. King would make a solo return visit to Atlantic before long. By then others were also furnishing The Drifters with hits but the Latin beat was never far away. Right at the end of 1960 King had recorded, under his own name, an overtly Hispanic song written by Jerry Leiber and Phil Spector. 'Spanish Harlem' was a melodically startling number about a beautiful girl in a harsh cityscape setting, but it was an utterly hypnotic song. Reminiscent of the *Valencia* section of Ibert's *Escales* and laced with Spanish guitar, marimba, and drum-beats, it eclipsed its intended A-side ('First Taste Of Love' written by Doc Pomus and Phil Spector) and even though King disliked it, it made his name as a solo artist and has been recorded hundreds of times all over the world.

During the first part of 1961 all was not well with the increasingly successful song writing partnership of Pomus and Shuman. When 'Surrender' (backed with their incomparably superior 'Little Sister') became a global hit in February of that year, Doc and Mort got the imprimatur of preferred suppliers of songs to the Elvis trade. He was the most famous act in the world and the money started rolling in, the Aberbachs became multi-millionaires, Doc and Mort's pay skyrocketed... and yet the writing was on the wall for the hitmakers. For the time being, despite Mort's frequent absences, they would go on to write other major hits, not only for Elvis and The Drifters but for several other artists. Particularly notable in 1961 was Del Shannon's first album rushed out to capitalise on his enormous hit 'Runaway'. It included three Pomus-Shuman songs, amongst them one superb number that would be eclipsed by Presley's version recorded a month later. 'Misery' and 'Wide Wide World' were both strong songs. Shannon would later go on to record Pomus-Shuman's 'Ginny In The Mirror' and a tweaked version of their Drifters song, originally called 'She Never Talked To Me That Way' but retitled for him as 'She Never Talked About Me' and improved in the process.

Mort kept on disappearing without warning but Doc, older, a family man and no traveller, made a virtue out of a necessity and was driven between the Hill & Range cubicle, home in Lynbrook or, during the week, at The Forrest Hotel. Gregarious, but preferring to be a hub for others to be drawn to, he had chosen The Forrest, almost opposite The Brill Building on West 49th Street. It was cheap and, perhaps more importantly, to some extent it recreated the bohemian lobby culture of The Broadway Central, attracting another concentration of what country songwriter Billy Joe Shaver characterised in a different context as 'lovable losers and no-account boozers'. When novelist Nick Hornby collaborated with Ben Folds on a tribute album to Doc Pomus he chose to focus on Doc's relatively brief sojourn at The Forrest for the song that bore his name. It name-checked a lot of Pomus-Shuman hits and offered a word-sketch of the man:

Man in a wheelchair listens to the chatter
Writes down all the insane crap he hears
He can't move around but it doesn't really matter
In the Forrest all you need is eyes and ears

The song also names a few of the principal lobby characters: Fred Neil, Jack Benny, Phil Spector, Pumpkin Juice, Eydie Gormé, Damon Runyon Jr. and members of The Duke Ellington orchestra.

Fred Neil was a Greenwich Village folk singer who became famous for writing *Midnight Cowboy*'s 'Everybody's Talkin''. He was married to Hill & Range's secretary Elaine, a frequent visitor from the other side of the street as Doc sat in The Forrest lobby holding court, taking notes and working. She would redirect people there when Doc was not in his Hill & Range office. Songs still got written, sometimes with the dependably undependable Mortie, but also with Phil Spector, already a weird fantasist who affected theatrical costumes. Steve Lawrence (Sidney Leibowitz) and Eydie Gormé (Edith Gormezano) were a durable husband and wife pop duo, graduates of a jazzy big band background, and although they might sound like another simpatico blending of Latin and Jewish qualities, Eydie too was Jewish and in fact a cousin of Neil Sedaka.

Among the petty criminals, con artists and assorted misfits one stood out as a legend in his own right. John Leslie McFarland (the real name of 'Pumpkin Juice') was another Paul Case-sponsored songwriter and one who could most kindly be called eccentric although he was probably certifiably insane. Stories of his heroic drinking, colourful criminality and doomed scams had made him a legend. He had allegedly once stolen a jumbo jet, taken a mummy from a New York museum, transporting it on the bus, stolen a police horse and ridden it the wrong way down a one-way Manhattan street and, naked, indulged in sex with a young woman in a snowstorm in the middle of 49th Street. The stories became part of the music industry's folklore and were no doubt embellished in their multiple retellings.

Perhaps a more reliable testimony to the eccentricity of J. Leslie McFarland (the use of his first name initial sometimes resulted in his being incorrectly credited as Jay Leslie McFarland) can be found in a list of some of his songs many of which had titles or lyrics that so clearly made them unusable that it remains a mystery how he produced so many that actually were published and sometimes even successful. He could never see them as being different from one another. Perhaps he was right – after all his 'Wang Dang Taffy-Apple Tango' which he co-wrote with Aaron Schroeder was picked up and actually recorded by Pat Boone in 1959. Louis Jordan recorded '(You Dyed Your Hair) Chartreuse' composed by McFarland and Billy Moore. 'Pigalle Love' ('I met a girl/in Paris, France/While at a rockin'/Pigalle dance…') was all McFarland's own work and it was recorded by Memphis Slim. Mort Shuman recalled that John Leslie was just as likely to write a song that consisted of nothing more than a shopping list of boys' and girls' names (Ted went out with Sue, Louise went out with Jim and so on) and then wonder why no one wanted it. He once used the pseudonym Johnny Jungletree when he recorded an album of tropically themed songs and the name lived on alongside Pumpkin Juice (the title of one of his children's songs) as one of the nicknames favoured by those who thought J. Leslie McFarland sounded like a name for a bank manager, not a mixed-race alcoholic with a twisted song writing talent.

Pumpkin Juice's alcohol-fuelled attempts to get a handout from music publishers when times were hard usually consisted of repeatedly turning up at their offices with his arm in a sling – however it was quite likely to be a different arm from day to day. Even so the same J. Leslie McFarland wrote 'Stuck On You' with Aaron Schroeder to give Elvis his first number one hit after coming out of the army. He also wrote 'Little Children' with Mort Shuman, a big hit for Billy J. Kramer in both Britain and America. One of the McFarland stories involved Doc who actually believed John Leslie when he said he had found Jesus, was giving up drink and going straight. As a result Doc secured him a rock bottom rate on a room at The Forrest whose lobby McFarland promptly assaulted with a stolen fire axe during his first – and last – drunken night's residency there. (One wonders, belatedly, what a big star like Jack Benny was doing in a joint like The Forrest. … unless his on-stage affectation for being a tightwad was not an affectation after all.)

Without formally acknowledging the incipient disintegration of the Pomus-Shuman hit machine, Paul Case had already started to try to encourage Doc to pair up with other songwriters, beginning with Phil Spector. Mort would usually return sooner or later, and maybe, with help, Doc could maintain the output in the interim. Jordan 'Jerry' Ragovoy was another potential co-writer although the main fruit of this collaboration seemed to surface quite some time later, when, co- writing under the name of Norman Meade, he helped Doc write a title song for Presley's insipid 1965 *Girl Happy* movie after a Pomus-Shuman attempt had been rejected. Mort Shuman contributed nothing at all to that film's dozen songs. Doc also collaborated on one song with the very young Ellie Greenwich, a musically gifted kid hailing from Brooklyn via Long Island. Before long she would team up with Jeff Barry to become half of a husband-and-wife song writing team to rival Goffin-King and Mann-Weil.

By late spring of 1961 Paul Case had acceded to a request from his friend Thomas 'Snuff' Garrett, an LA-based producer at Liberty Records in Hollywood with a roster of artists that included Bobby Vee, Johnny Burnette, Gene McDaniels and Gary Lewis & The Playboys. Seeking material for his protégé Bobby Vee (Robert Velline) Garrett asked if Doc could come out to LA for a spell. Doc hated the idea of flying again especially to write for another teen idol called Bobby, but he went and was duly installed on Hollywood Boulevard at The Roosevelt Hotel (prompting perhaps a wry recollection of his youthful sojourn at Roosevelt's Warm Springs spa?). Unexpectedly Mort Shuman turned up there too, redirected from New York when he put in a sudden reappearance at Hill & Range. In between Mort's good-time sorties down to Mexico and after some unsuccessful writing attempts for Vee, the pair met up with their old friend Bobby Darin, now also LA-based and recently married to 'Gidget' and 'Tammy' film star Sandra Dee. ('Look at Me I'm Sandra Dee!' was a satirical song from *Grease*, mocking its heroine's wholesome image). Doc and Mort offered Darin two songs originally intended for Bobby Vee but rejected by Garrett because they were too 'rock'n'roll'. Darin the musical chameleon who had proved himself a supreme pop singer with 'Dream Lover' somehow failed to know what to do with them and passed on them too. Back in New York Doc and Mort handed their double rejects to Paul Case who submitted them to Elvis Presley's camp. 'Surrender', which had been released in February, had gone to number one and stayed in the charts for weeks, so Pomus-Shuman's stock was high with Presley. Presley's people snapped up both of the new songs: 'Little Sister' and '(Marie's The Name) His Latest Flame'. The latter had appeared on Del Shannon's debut album just before Presley's version was released but no one had recorded 'Little Sister'. Many would.

"We wrote 'Little Sister' in The Hotel Roosevelt in Hollywood," Mort Shuman recalled. "I had a guitar with me and I started fooling around with a riff which had nothing to do with the rhythm on Elvis' record. I had a very fast, driving guitar thing going and Elvis slowed it down by half. Doc came up with his inimitable R&B classic lyrics, which are really great. 'Little Sister' is among the Elvis records that I love best, and Ry Cooder did a cover version that was different again and I loved that too…. I also love Dwight Yoakam's version…which was a big country hit."

'Little Sister' was also the song to which LaVern Baker recorded an 'answer'. They tried to call it 'Hey Elvis' but there were objections. It was released as 'Hey Memphis'.

Of '(Marie's The Name) His Latest Flame' Mort simply said. "I can't deny it – I stole Bo Diddley's riff (even though) we get to the middle eight where the song breaks and becomes something totally different." In their turn The Smiths would steal from 'His Latest Flame'. In 1985 they decanted a couple of verses into the introduction of 'Rusholme Ruffians' because Johnny Marr loved the song which had been in his parents' record collection. "But from being a kid I noticed how many other songs had that chord change," he recalled. "When Morrissey sang it, it sounded really brilliant."

Thanks to a French RCA double album titled 'Elvis Chante Mort Shuman & Doc Pomus' (note the reversal of names!) and its inclusion on mort.shuman.com's Music/Audio page it is still possible to hear Mort's demo of the song. Characterised by his assured vocal and some intriguing, impossible-to-analyse distortion of the piano in that middle eight, it somehow identifies Mort Shuman as the ascending star of the partnership. Presley's camp called him in the middle of the night when they heard that particular demo and asked him how he got that piano sound. He had no idea, it was an unintended effect.

Their double-sided Presley single was not the last of Doc and Mort's staggering run of 13 hits for the year but they were probably their two finest songs of a vintage spell. It was only appropriate that at a time when a break-up looked imminent Doc Pomus and Mort Shuman should write two truly great songs that were given a superb treatment by the most popular singer in the world. For many fans Elvis would rarely hit those heights again and, ironically, Doc and Mort's last joint song for him would be 'Double Trouble', the title song for yet another dismal movie. (Mort always had difficulty recalling that song, sometimes claiming he had nothing to do with it, but it remains credited to Pomus-Shuman.) In 1969 Mort really was the sole writer of 'You'll Think Of Me', the flipside of Elvis' 'Suspicious Minds' released in 1970 and a more fitting farewell composition for The King who had just four more singles to go and barely seven years to live.

Back in 1961, Pomus and Shuman's *annus mirabilis* at The Brill Building, there was as yet no indication of the imminent invasion that would shift the axis of pop music from mid-town Broadway to Liverpool and London. There were, however, indications that Mort's future interests lay far from New York City. He rather fancied himself as a singer (and his terrific demo of '[Marie's The Name] His Latest Flame' proved he was entitled to do so), but he claimed that the Aberbachs and Doc wanted to keep him writing "so they gave him BIG cash bonuses and extended the contract". In the end it still wasn't enough. Imperceptibly Doc's reign as the senior partner had been eroded. Mort, still only in his mid-twenties, was now not just an equal partner but the dominant one.

7

Degrees Of Separation

If 1961 saw at least 25 Pomus–Shuman songs being recorded, their 1962 tally was less than half that number. Two were the Del Shannon sides already mentioned, 'Ginny In The Mirror', a so-so song, and 'You Never Talked About Me'. The latter was an energetic and slightly modified version of the song The Drifters recorded as 'You Never Talked To Me That Way' and it suited Shannon's falsetto vocal breaks and trademark instrumental break on the 'Musitron', that incisive forerunner of the analogue synthesizer which had helped make 'Runaway' such a distinctive hit. Doc and Mort wrote three numbers for Elvis including the sublime 'Suspicion', an album song that would become a hit single for Terry Stafford in 1964, and which in 1970 was recorded by Vivian Stanshall, late of The Bonzo Dog Doo-Dah Band, whose deliberately melodramatic reading was produced by, of all people, Who drummer Keith Moon. Another 1962 Pomus and Shuman composition was the retro, raucous 'Seven Day Weekend' for Gary 'US' Bonds, all of which contributed to a respectable haul but the team's output was nevertheless diminishing, mainly due to Mort's increasing absences. 'She's Not You', was an Elvis summer hit written by Doc in collaboration with Leiber and Stoller who could see that

Mort's dereliction of duty was leaving Doc languishing, professionally at least. At home in Lynbrook, Long Island he was preoccupied with the July arrival of Geoffrey, his second child with Willi. By autumn both needed a break and the family travelled to Florida. With his working partnership with Mort patchy at best, quite what Doc was taking a break from was unclear (although one thing that was clear was Doc's temperamental dissatisfaction with the quiet domestic life). Willi had started to build herself a career in musicals, becoming pregnant with Geoffrey during the run of *Fiorello!* (a musical about New York City's 99th mayor, Fiorello La Guardia) in which she played his first wife Thea Almerigotti.

Throughout 1962 Doc's only contact with Mort alternated between short, usually impatient song writing sessions and the arrival of letters that sported a bewildering array of international postmarks. The contents of these letters might reflect on their most recent falling out, although Mort unfailingly wrote to Doc in very affectionate terms, acknowledging his own immaturity and venturing to hope that Doc still felt warmly about him too. "I've been with you longer than your wife has," he pointed out in one letter, "so take that into account, coupled with the fact that I'm still growing up." It was an innocently ominous comparison, underscoring the fact that Doc's two main partners were looking like baling out.

★ ★ ★

Nineteen sixty-three produced nine recorded songs of which one of the biggest successes was a number reviled by its singer. Mort Shuman always resented Andy Williams' contempt for 'Can't Get Used To Losing You' which is in fact a very imaginative Pomus-Shuman song with an edgy, pizzicato rhythm interspersed with more flowing romantic sections. It was the A-side of a single whose B-side was Henry Mancini's syrupy and inappropriate theme song for *The Days Of Wine And Roses*, a hard-hitting black-and-white movie about alcoholism. Williams actually went on his TV show and prefaced his performance of 'Can't Get Used To Losing You' – then number one in America – by saying it was the B-side of his new single. Mort later said, "I don't like to badmouth but sometimes you really have to because otherwise the public thinks that everybody is nice and everybody is sweet. Well, dear public, not everybody is. Andy Williams had such disdain for the song. Why? He's entitled to his opinion but then, why record it?"

Mort's major 1963 adventure was a significant one. On the pretext of atoning to his ageing widowed mother Esther for whom Morty's adolescence had been such a trying time, the now-wealthy young song writer took her to Israel to see her closest childhood friend from Poland, a woman who had survived Auschwitz and was now living with her husband in the Jewish state that was technically 12 years younger that Mortimer Shuman himself. Once there Mort soon left her to reminisce in Tel Aviv and set off on a walking tour of the country which provided him with just as many opportunities to raise hell and chase women as anywhere else. He met a woman on a kibbutz and characterised her as a Sabra, a loaded word that connotes a Jew born in Israel and who, like the native Sabra plant (prickly pear), is rough on the outside but soft on the inside. Mort encountered some difficulties with her father after trying to compare her exterior and interior textures by the empirical method and left the kibbutz after three days returning to Tel-Aviv via the Galilee and the Gaza Strip.

One of Mort's 1991 recollections gives a full flavour of the next phase of the adventure: "One night (I) went to the Jaffa, the Arab twin city which was becoming an area for many of the creative people in Israel. And (I) got (my) first gig singing and playing in a club for food and drinks. And (I) played with Willie Dixon and Memphis Slim and had the owner's wife thrown in. Sometimes it was rock. Sometimes it was folk, sometimes it was jazz. But what more could (I) want than eating a pork sandwich on Pitta bread with a beer overlooking the Bay of Jaffa with the minarets silhouetted against the eternal sky and whispering sweet nothings in Yiddish?"

Back in Philadelphia Freddy Cannon (Frederick Anthony Picariello Jr.) had recorded, perhaps appropriately, 'The Ups And Downs Of Love', a decidedly minor Pomus and Shuman composition that like Del Shannon's version of 'You Never Talked About Me' found its way into one of three weirdly incpt British pop music films produced by Milton Subotsky. Perhaps the bottom of the barrel was being scraped because Mort was not around much in '62 and '63 to help Doc fill it up. In any event when Mort did return to New York ('You'd think Tin Pan Alley would disappear if (I) didn't get on the first plane') it was clear that he was a looking for another distraction and kept avoiding work until it turned up.

Distraction duly appeared in the shape of one Esther Thobi at Café Sahbra, a nightclub in Manhattan's Westover Hotel on West 72nd Street. Both the venue and the chanteuse were ominously named. Sahbra was an alternative spelling of the name for the prickly/soft plant, while Esther was of course also his mother's name. No doubt Mort would have ignored the piece of traditional Jewish wisdom about not marrying a woman with your mother's name even if he had known about it. Still inebriated by his good times in Israel he was so struck with Esther Thobi's dark beauty that he married her in New York in May of 1963 and repeated the ceremony for her parents in Jerusalem soon afterwards. Their union would last less than a year and in the interim Mort and Esther's fiery clashes were epic, unyielding and unpleasant. When a chastened Mort downed drinks and told his outrageous tales of marital conflict to Doc and Willi out in Lynbrook, one wonders whether Doc thought ruefully of Millie and Morris' long war of attrition and how their lives might have turned out differently if only they had managed to fall out as spectacularly and finally as Mort and Esther had. The divorce, when it came, had an unintended consequence for Doc's lawyer brother Raoul who, with absolutely no experience in divorce law, was persuaded to represent Mort and managed to pull off a theatrical courtroom triumph when he 'proved' Esther's infidelity by producing a coached (and almost certainly bribed) witness to say that he had slept with her. Her alimony was dramatically cut to 20% of what she had been asking and Raoul's future reputation as an ace divorce lawyer was assured.

Doc was heading downhill through 1964 and 1965. The two main relationships in his life, with Willi and with Mort, were slowly disintegrating. Both parties had grown up in thrall of Doc but after eight or nine years of marriage Willi was now a mother and a working actress, often away touring. Mort, his apprentice days long behind him, was being recognised for his extraordinary talent, if not in the US then abroad, particularly in England which was becoming his favourite port of call now that the swinging sixties were underway. France's rockers were also quick to record French language versions of some classic Pomus and Shuman hits and many versions of 'Save The Last Dance For Me' were recorded as 'Garde La Dernière Danse Pour Moi' by artists ranging from *petite anglaise* ex-pat Petula Clark, through rocker Eddy Mitchell (Claude Moine) to the exotic Egyptian-Italian-French chanteuse Dalida (Iolanda Cristina Gigliotti). What Doc and the Brill Building habitués saw as a dispiriting British invasion of their New York patch, Mort was sporadically enjoying first-hand in London, hanging out with The Rolling Stones manager Andrew Loog Oldham, Mick and Keith and Marianne Faithfull.

Doc was putting on weight and becoming less and less mobile. If Mort became any more mobile he would probably burn up. Doc gave up drink but continued to smoke heavily. Mort gave up nothing. Doc gravitated more and more towards The Forrest where the cavalcade of characters was never-ending and he could hold court in the lobby or in his room. He tried to groom a young singer from the Virgin Isles called Scotty Fagan as a performer, perhaps to sublimate a need to mentor someone now that Mort was all grown up. Willi started to take Sharon and Geoffrey on tours when her roles in musicals demanded it. For Doc a pattern was emerging that had started when he had insisted on rejecting the Aberbachs' offer of an elegant penthouse office with a view in favour of a windowless cubby hole. At the time it looked like a strategy to discourage Mort from distraction, but in retrospect it seems as if Doc had perhaps simply become too used to fantasising about success and that when his dreams came true – the money, the beautiful woman and the middle-class home on Long Island – he became restless for the trappings of the struggle again. This was surely not going to end well.

Even so, 1964's thin crop of half-a dozen Pomus and Shuman songs did include the exuberant and deceptively well-crafted 'Viva Las Vegas' which 30 years later would receive a slow and hypnotically haunting treatment from Shawn Colvin, one of the many musicians who had turned to Doc for advice when starting out. Irma Thomas' '(I'm) Gonna Cry Til My Tears Run Dry' was from Doc and his protégé Scotty Fagan, but 'Wrong For Each Other' saw Doc and Mort in harness again, giving the perennially ungrateful Andy Williams another great song even if its chord sequences bore a passing resemblance to another hit Mort wrote in the same year, this time with the dependably unstable J. Leslie McFarland: 'Little Children'. That song underscored Mort's fame in Britain since it marked a departure from the Lennon & McCartney songs that at the time were being offered to Billy J. Kramer (William Ashton) & The Dakotas, another of the Brian Epstein-managed Liverpool acts that were springing up like mushrooms post-Beatlemania. Kramer's George Martin-produced version was a hit both in the UK and the US. On one of his frequent 1960s trips to London Mort even recorded for Andrew Loog Oldham – as Mort Shuman III – an almost unrecognisable cod-classical keyboard version of 'Little Children', a session about which he could later remember little.

★   ★   ★

For Doc his two marriages, personal and professional, were effectively over by the autumn of 1965. He was 40 years old and, being a well-read man, may have been wondering about F. Scott Fitzgerald's famous line from *The Last Tycoon*, 'There are no second acts in American lives'. If he did, perhaps he was persuaded that Fitzgerald was right, because consciously or otherwise, he set about replaying his own first act, recasting The Forrest as the new The Broadway Central where he had first met and wooed Willi. Now he was established as The Forrest lobby's resident attraction, an increasingly obese and immobile Sage of The Blues who, in his own words, wrote songs 'for those who stumble in the night'.

He was already trying to make history repeat itself. With ambitions to manage Scott Fagan he had set up Pomshu Productions. A quixotic venture having hardly more substance than the chimeric R&B Records, Pomshu then made a second and possibly final signing: a short-lived girl trio of fifteen year-old Jewish schoolgirls – Joanna DeClemente, Louise Robbins and Linda Stern – called The Lovelites. Perhaps revealing more about Doc's appetite for being a father figure to young girls than she intended, Louise Robbins recalled: "We worked with Doc at The Forrest Hotel... He rarely walked in those days and stayed in his hotel room during the week... We also worked with Mortie Shuman, but not as much as with Doc. He was protective and nurturing as well as demanding and professional about what he wanted from our talents. We'd be in that hotel room for hours rehearsing."

The Lovelites' career unravelled when they fell within the orbit of Phil Spector although their now ultra-rare recording 'He's My Eddie Baby' which is revered by girl group fanatics, only ever appeared on a demo disc from Associated Record Studios on Seventh Avenue at 48th Street, the place where Mort had recorded demos for submission to Elvis. Louise Robbins thinks they may have recorded this for Doc before Spector's involvement.

The déjà-vu theme continued. When a pair of 18-year old co-eds from the Midwest arrived in the suite next to Doc's room, there were unavoidable echoes of Willi and Bobby's first appearance at the Broadway Central. Doc was (again) attracted to the blonde. Her name was Shirlee Hauser and she effectively re-enacted Willi's youthful fascination with Doc, 22 years her senior, a father figure who seemed to be held in awe as a songwriter, who seemed to hold a pass-key to the most thrilling venues of the demi-monde and who simply seemed authoritative, shockingly honest and strangely compelling. Shirlee too was an aspiring actress.

Pomus and Shuman had no hits in 1965 and the last knockings of their mutual output would emerge in 1966, the year Paul Case refused to renew their contract. For Doc it looked like a disaster and it was accompanied by another when he suffered a bad fall in the street and tore the ligaments in both knees. He was hospitalised, eventually returning to The Forrest six weeks after his fall and already resigning himself to abandoning his crutches altogether and using a wheelchair for most trips.

Mort met Willi for dinner at Doc's behest; he was supposed to try to talk her out of divorcing Doc but Mort was a bad choice because he was looking to do the same thing. It was sad but for Mort it looked like freedom. He'd made a million dollars from song writing with Doc who probably made considerably more. Despite the usual song writers' cross-trading where here and there Doc used to suggest a melody line or Mort a lyric, Mort Shuman had been the music man and only the most biased observer could pretend that it was Doc's words rather than his tunes that had won over Elvis and the young rock'n'roll fans. Many years later Mort would say without rancour that Doc had not always given him the credit he was due but he would always love his old pal and always did his best to speak fairly about him.

Certainly neither could have had their particular first success without the other but while Doc had written a handful of truly classic lyrics and very many more workmanlike ones that showed that he was a craftsman writing for money, Mort was endlessly inventive and took a certain pride in fashioning hit melodies. Hardly less aware of the value of a buck than Doc and not what you might call a disciplined worker either, Mort felt it was an endorsement of his work when Elvis copied something from one of his demos even though he was genuinely unimpressed by the supposed honour of writing for The King. "I couldn't care less," he later said. "In those days I was really quite a rebellious kind of guy, pretty much knocking most of

Jerome Felder a.k.a. Doc Pomus performing in a Greenwich Village club in the mid-1950s.

The start of memorable partnership: Shuman and Pomus in the late 1950s, two Jewish songwriters dutifully posing in front of an incongruous display of Christmas cards in this Hill & Range publicity shot. MICHAEL OCHS ARCHIVES/GETTY IMAGES

Left: The Mystics, for whom Doc & Mort wrote 'Teenager In Love' even though their label bosses gave it to Dion & The Belmonts instead. The Mystics still had a major hit with a hasty replacement Pomus & Shuman song 'Hushabye'. MICHAEL OCHS ARCHIVES/GETTY IMAGES Right: Young man in a hurry. Teen idol Bobby Darin in performance, the suit and the body language already signalling his impatience to become the new Sinatra. GAB ARCHIVE/REDFERNS

Constance Ockelman, a Brooklynite who, as Veronica Lake, had enjoyed brief but dazzling fame as a Hollywood star before a sad decline into schizophrenia and alcoholism. She helped Doc prop up a few Brooklyn bars on her way down.

Blues singer and Pomus buddy Otis Blackwell was working as a Brooklyn tailor's assistant until he struck gold by writing a string of songs for Elvis Presley starting with 'Don't Be Cruel' and 'All Shook Up'. This 1969 studio portrait shows Blackwell pretending to write a song in front of a poster of his most illustrious client. GILLES PETARD/REDFERNS

'The Drifters' was a brand name for an ever-changing cast of vocalists — over 60 different performers in all. This 1959 shot shows the second line-up which many consider to be the definitive one: L-R: Charlie Thomas, Ben E. King, Dock Green and Elsbeary Hobbs.
MICHAEL OCHS ARCHIVES/GETTY IMAGES

Shuman performs at The Olympia in his adopted city of Paris during the summer of 1976. RICHARD MELLOUL/SYGMA/CORBIS

Always at home in show business, Mort (left) parties with broadcast journalist Michel Drucker, comedian Thierry Le Luron and legendary chanteuse Mireille Mathieu. BERTRAND RINDOFF PETROFF/GETTY IMAGES

Mort Shuman poses in the Bois de Boulogne during a photo shoot for his 1980 French album *Slave (Slav)*.

Mort at the piano rehearsing a number for a 1976 TV show with singer Dani (Danièle Graule) and actress Nathalie Delon, ex-wife of French film star Alain Delon. JEAN TESSEYRE/PARIS MATCH VIA GETTY IMAGES

Housebound Doc celebrates a birthday with his old buddy and idol Big Joe Turner. STEPHANIE CHERNIKOWSKI/REDFERNS

the whole scene, quite critical of a lot of that stuff. I suffered from a laid-back kind of attitude. Everybody was trying to make millions of dollars back in those days. I was only making about a million I guess, and it was much more fun to go out and do all sorts of funny things with girls, stay high on various kinds of herbs, various beverages, stuff like that. That's pretty much the way it was. I'm not a driven man. And on top of all that I never met (Elvis). Never got a phone call, never got a Christmas card. Nothing!"

Doc could probably not bring himself to admit that replacing Mort was not going to be as easy as replacing Willi but all attempts to write hits with other Brill Building composers came to little or nothing. He finally came across a man called Johnny Mel who would become his new partner even though he had never written (and never would write) a note of music. What Johnny partnered Doc in was playing high stakes poker, taking him to games and coaching him, in so doing giving him an entrée into a world that occupied him and kept some money coming in for many years, on and off. Soon Doc would realise that the only way to any guarantee income was to host the games himself, a move that further reinforced his drift towards immobility and took over the home he had bought in Manhattan after abandoning another sequence of hotel rooms. He shared it with Shirlee who was seemingly still reading from Willi's script, nagging him about his health and weight. She was no great fan of the poker meetings that tended to turn home sweet home into a smoky, pot-scented bar. When Doc's divorce from Willi came through he found he had to give most of the proceeds of the sale of the Long Island house to the Internal Revenue having neglected – dyed-in-the-wool bluesman that he was – to pay them anything at all out of his considerable earnings of the previous eight years or so.

While Doc's slow decline was beginning, the last Pomus-Shuman song was released, 'Double Trouble' from the reliably awful Elvis film of the same name. Mort was already becoming committed to the life of a playboy, hanging out with the advance troops of the British invasion – Dudley Moore who was in the Broadway run of *Beyond*

The Fringe, Albert Finney who triumphed in the 1963 film *Tom Jones*. In 1964 The Beatles arrived in America and their influence, added to that of Bob Dylan, assured Mort and almost everybody else that so-called Brill Building-type two-and-a-half-minute catchy pop songs were being replaced with something quite different. Bob Dylan in particular was rewiring the agenda of popular music for a new generation, writing and performing songs that might last for the whole side of an album and mixing social protest with hymns to personal emotional freedom. 'Teenager In Love' it wasn't.

Mort travelled in the French Antilles where, as he put it, his favourite climate combined with his favourite food 'to calm his turbulent spirit'. He kept returning to London, hanging out with Ray and Dave Davies, Julie Driscoll, Eric Burdon, Alan Price, Jimi Hendrix and The Small Faces for whom he co-wrote 'Sha La La Lee' with the kind of black musician even he had never encountered before – Stepney-born entertainer Kenny Lynch. Mort remembered going to Lynch's house in Fulham where his host told Mort that he couldn't write rock'n'roll anymore. Rising to the bait Shuman knocked off 'Sha La La Lee' in about 20 minutes and his friendship with Andrew Loog Oldham, who owned Immediate Records, resulted in The Small Faces snapping it up. Another collaboration with Lynch produced an outstanding hit for Cilla Black (Priscilla White), 'Love's Just A Broken Heart', a terrifically dramatic song which sounds very French in an up-and-down-the-scale sort of way. This was because Mort originally wrote the melody with a French lyric writer Michele Vendome when the song was called 'L'Amour Est Ce Qu'il Est' so she shared the writing credit with Mort and Kenny. He even tried his hand at arranging Cilla Black's recorded performance of the song, courtesy of George Martin. Back in New York Mort was now belatedly studying at the Conservatory "So I was now very much into counterpoint and harmony," he recalled, "but I was never really very good at it… anyway we did go into the big EMI studios and I was shaking my arms around as if I was Herbert von Karajan with the strings going up and down.

So I did arrange that, and also the other one she did, 'What Good Am I?'.".

'What Good Am I?' and its B-side 'Over My Head' were also Shuman/Lynch songs, although the latter sounded curiously like a Bacharach-David pastiche, a love child of 'What's New Pussycat?' and 'Do You Know The Way To San Jose?' Mort also co-wrote 'Here I Go Again' for The Hollies with British writer Clive Westlake who had written several songs for Dusty Springfield.

Additionally Mort found time to write three songs for one of those cheap 1960s movie musicals the British used to make that made you rather wish they wouldn't. *Every Day's A Holiday* (*Seaside Swingers* in the US) required songs that reflected the plot like a stage musical so its title number and two others – 'Romeo Jones' and 'Cor Blimey' – were never destined for the charts. Mort wrote them with Clive Westlake and Kenny Lynch and the only thing of note about this let's-do-the-show-right-here movie was that its cinematography was by Nicolas Roeg, five years before he co-directed *Performance* and a decade's worth of very impressive if controversial films.

Paris and Cannes vied with London and the French Antilles for Mort's attentions and even he could never quite remember the frequency or sequence of his '60s travel schedule. Here his hastily assembled notes for the autobiography he would never write sound appropriately impressionistic and breathless:

"… he [again meaning himself] met a little model who was lost and suicidal and she finally did try to commit suicide in his flat while he was away.... It inspired him to write a song.... he met an interesting woman who was locked in a body brace which inhibited movement. Mort had to try it, which he did. The affair ended when she got better. Then the parties in New York with all the beautiful people, especially at Eileen Ford's house with the top world models floating around. Mort had his share of them, followed them from collection to collection in Rome and Paris. Life became a glass of champagne and Mort was more and more dissolute. He lived for a while with a top American model and started writing some songs with Jerry Ragovoy, one of the top soul writer-producers of that time. Mort and Doc had practically stopped writing. It's sad but that's life. Then on a trip to Paris, Mort met Eddie Barclay who took him under his wing. Eddie was one of the great swingers of all time and life was a fête. Pot was gone but poppers and Black Russians were there and tho' he escaped the hard stuff, many others were not so lucky. Like Jim Morrison and Jimi and Janis Joplin for all of whom Jerry Ragovoy and Mort started writing. Mort also found time to fall in love again, this time in Hamburg. It ended sadly for Mort and he drowned his sorrows in Maltesers and Urguell in every dive and house on the Reeperbahn and it just goes to show that favourite things, things you love the most, sometimes evolve from unhappy, desperate experiences. Nowhere was he sadder than in Hamburg and yet it remains one of his favourite places.... Back to New York and the discos and the parties and to the morning afters. And the abortions and weekends in the Caribbean. The night they invented champagne went on for two years and you must excuse him if some details were hazy and the chronological order is not exact. Life wasn't very logical in those days."

In St Tropez where Barclay had a house he and Mort wrote a few songs one summer and some of them were recorded. Dinners were extravagant and dinner guests likewise, with movie and music celebrities including Jean-Paul Belmondo, Charles Aznavour and Alain Delon.

"And then one day someone made (me) listen to Jacques Brel," Mort recalled, "And (I) saw the light. All became clear and clean and bright once again. And (I) knew what (I) had to do. (I) went to see Brel perform, became his number one groupie, followed him on tour, bought all his records and flew home to translate Brel's songs into English for America."

Looking back to this epiphany Mort Shuman said: "In those days I was always searching for something, I was never satisfied. You go into the depths of debauchery and degradation and things like that trying exorcise the demons... and all that! I was going through this consciousness crisis, all that silly stuff that everybody goes through when they're young. I started bumming around the Continent – bumming in five-star hotels, but bumming – and all of a sudden I heard the songs of this guy who had the virility and power in his voice like the black soul singers, like Wilson Pickett or Otis and singing what I guess people would call poetry. Very simple melodic structures but very very powerful, and talking about things that were meaningful: about old age about prostitutes, about war. Not 'message' songs in our Anglo-Saxon sense like we're going to San Francisco or ban the bomb type things – it was much more general outlook on the human condition. I just got knocked over by it and had finally found a reason again in life. What I was going to do was translate all these songs and bring them to the English-speaking public. Not that Jacques himself could have cared less! He was not very much of an Anglophile and he didn't care what Rod McKuen was doing with his songs or what Eric Blau and I (eventually) did with them."

In a way Californian Rod McKuen had pre-empted Mort Shuman by discovering Brel earlier and creating English versions of some of his songs. However McKuen's version of 'If You Go Away' (based on Brel's song 'Ne Me Quitte Pas') and particularly 'Seasons In The Sun'(based on Brel's 'Le Moribond') which became a '70s pop hit for Terry Jacks, were less translations and more English lyrics that only very broadly echoed the sense of the originals.

At the time Jacques Brel (Jacques Romain Georges Brel) was known only to a comparatively small cliques of enthusiasts outside France and his native Belgium where he was born in 1929. He was French-speaking although of Flemish ancestry, and at the age of 24 he was encouraged to move to Paris with his young wife and two children after signing a record deal with Philips. There he worked hard to support himself and his family while he waited for his career to take off, living at a hotel and giving guitar lessons to pay his rent and supplement work on the cabaret circuit. After a heavy spell of touring Brel's wife and children left Paris and returned to Belgium. He continued to undertake a heavy working schedule and In 1960, his new impresario, Charles Marouani, organised a series of international concert tours that took him to the Middle East, the Soviet Union, Canada, and the United States. It was during this period that Mort discovered him and flew back to the US to begin his translating project. He would soon discover that while Brel was no longer unknown in America, he remained a minority taste, his French language songs still remaining a major barrier to wider recognition.

This period marked the start of Mortimer Shuman's comprehensive demolition of F. Scott Fitzgerald's pronouncement about American lives having no second act. It is no exaggeration to say that Mort Shuman's own life and its second act almost defy belief. In 1966 he was only just starting. By 1968 he and fellow American Milton Eric Blau had created a revue by translating some of Brel's songs into English and it opened at The Village Gate nightclub at the corner of Thompson and Bleecker in Manhattan's Greenwich Village. Called *Jacques Brel Is Alive And Well And Living In Paris* the show is still being staged, all over the world, 45 years later.

Soon Mort would join the ranks of that European phenomenon, the mature *chansonnier*. Brel himself of course. Georges Brassens. Serge Gainsbourg. Paolo Conti. Hugues Aufray. Guy Béart. Light years (as well as actual years) away from all those teenage Bobbys – Vee, Rydell, Vinton and the rest – these men sang about real, imperfect lives: love, hopes, dreams and death. In a couple of years' time Mort Shuman would try to do the same and in doing so he would go to the number one spot in the French charts with his very first attempt.

8

Alive and Well...

"Wandering Jew, reckless like a Slav, polished like an Italian, rocker and crooner, wise and extravagant, he blended innumerable influences around the same sensibility, intense, palpable and magnificent."

Only the French could come up with such a fulsome assessment of Mort Shuman. 'Only the French' is not an implied criticism but simply recognition of the fact that it was indeed only the French who really 'got' the Mort of the late 1960s and 1970s. The above comes from the blurb of a French book celebrating the man who shifted his allegiance from the US to France where he was welcomed with warmth that must baffle many American visitors to that country. Four more paragraphs follow the one quoted above, all equally adulatory: "... astonishing imagination and energy... juggler of sounds as well as words... his works, even today are spread across the entire planet...'. Doc Pomus is not mentioned once.

Mort went to France first as a frequent visitor, an enthusiastic fan of the cuisine and of course the wine, and intrigued that some of his songs with Doc had been translated and recorded by French performers. Richard Anthony (Ricardo Btesh) had a cosmopolitan background but recorded French versions of dozens of American and British hits from 1958 onwards, so perhaps it came as little surprise that in his rock'n'roll days he had embraced some of the Pomus-Shuman oeuvre. However, 'Save The Last Dance For Me' was quite a song in its own right and the French version was already becoming something of a standard there. In the late 1960s and afterwards other French rockers were more than happy to welcome collaborations with Mort. He wrote songs for French megastar Johnny Hallyday (Jean-Philippe Smet) and the tragically short-lived Mike Brant (Moshé Michaël Brand). Mort's friendship with record producer and label owner Eddie Barclay opened other doors too but, however indirectly, it was perhaps the earlier efforts of another French singing star, Hugues Aufray, that eventually prompted Mort to parlay his new found obsession with Jacques Brel into a memorable project. Aufray had become fascinated with Bob Dylan through what at the time was the common route of first hearing Peter, Paul & Mary's sweetened versions of his more accessible songs. With the help of Pierre Delanoë, Hugues Aufray adapted Dylan's radical songs for the French market, making an album of them.

Mort had first met Aufray on one of his frequent trips to Paris in late 1964 after being impressed by some lines in a song he had heard on French radio. The song was Aufray's 'Le Coeur Gros' ('The Heavy Heart'), a poetic list of scenes to depress the spirit (a lost dog in the city, an old and lonely Spanish Civil War survivor and so on). The verse in question referenced the funeral of the assassinated John F. Kennedy and revolved around the humanity of the burial as well as its political import:

When... you suddenly understood, my brother
That he was not just a president
You had a heavy heart

This, remember, was at about the time when The Beatles were riding high with 'I Feel Fine' in the UK, 'I Want To Hold Your

Hand' in the US and the Shuman-McFarland hit 'Little Children' was doing well on both sides of the Atlantic. (Aufray's muse, Dylan, was not at the time having any overwhelming impact on the Anglophone charts).

Wanting to know more about the man who put a slain US president into a popular song, Mort asked Lillian Konyn, then writing lyrics under the name of Vline Buggy (the pseudonym was a conscious conflation of the two separate pen names under which she [Buggy] and her recently deceased sister Evelyn [Vline] had written songs). A past collaborator with Aufray, Vline Buggy introduced the two and it was a meeting of minds and spirits.

"I met Mort Shuman at Place des Ternes at the wheel of magnificent Rolls and we had lunch together," Aufray recalls. "He presented me with some music that reflected his Slavic origins and for which I asked Vline to write me some words. Vline had lost a sister and I had lost a brother and so it was from that communal sadness that the idea of the song was born. That's how she presented me with the lyric of 'Céline' for this superb melody of Mort's."

Mort had already begun to look for ways of introducing Brel's unique musical worldview to American audiences. The language was a barrier (just ask Johnny Hallyday whose fame was colossal… but only in France and Francophone Québec) but language had never been much of an obstacle to polyglot Mort so he thought seriously about translating Brel's dark, awkward songs himself. It turned out not to be as easy as he thought; it was like translating poetry where meaning and style are so closely interwoven. Back in New York he consulted Nat Shapiro, Columbia Records' International Artists' Representative whom he learned was himself a Brel fan and had already been in touch with the Manhattan-based poet Eric Blau about Anglicizing the Belgian's compelling but intransigent songs of murder, betrayal, love and loss and the whole damn thing. Blau was married to musical performer and comedienne Elly Stone and she too was a Brel enthusiast. Encouraged by his wife, Blau had already translated three Brel songs ('Marieke', 'Crazy Carousel' and 'If You

Go Away') which found their way into her various revue-style stage appearances, notably Blau's first attempt at writing a musical revue, *O Oysters* (1961), which opened at The Village Gate in Greenwich Village. Elly co-starred with Jon Voight, still eight years shy of his star-making role as Joe Buck in *Midnight Cowboy* and 14 years away from giving the world a baby girl named Angelina Jolie Voight.

Between them Eric Blau, Mort Shuman and Elly Stone conspired with Nat Shapiro to bring into being another revue, this time dedicated to and shaped by the Anglicised songs of Jacques Brel. Blau said it was Shapiro who suggested its intentionally cumbersome title, mischievously bouncing off another one that was well-known at the time 'Adolf Hitler Is Alive and Well And Living In Argentina'.

Mort and Eric spent a long time playing and winnowing Brel's vast catalogue down to about 26 songs and translating them. Somewhere down the line Blau, whose poems had been published in France's leading poetry magazine *Poesie*, admitted that Mort's French was better than his. Mort, for his part, said, 'I suppose you could say I was just the midwife to Brel's music'. Perhaps, but at one point when Mort had been half-heartedly recording a few pop tracks under his own name in London ('Cry A Little', 'She Ain't Nothing', his pseudo-classical version of 'Little Children' and 'Monday Monday') he gave up that line of work altogether to concentrate on his new obsession, the Brel translations. On one occasion he rang Brel and explained that he had slowed down one of the master's songs to make it an easier fit with its English lyrics. Mort worriedly sang the new version over the phone to him. Brel replied, "You've made it better. Your version is better than mine" – a generous verdict although one that has to be seen in the context of Brel's general absence of interest in what others did to his songs.

In New York the show's original players were Elly Stone, Mort Shuman, Alice Whitfield and Shawn Elliott. It opened nervously at The Village Gate. The venue was not entirely welcoming in that it had wooden seats and poor sightlines. The audience didn't care and was galvanised by the performance. Mort now had a new *raison d'être*, sang as if his life depended on it and revealed unsuspected talents as a comic actor. Even so the show garnered mainly negative reviews and was confidently expected to lose $1,000 a week before closing. Heroically underwritten for a year at least by its enthusiastic principal producer Hank Hoffman (who need not have worried), it survived its first week and then triumphed, selling out for the next four years. It has today long since crossed that invisible line where periodically some show seems destined to be revived somewhere in the world forever.

Always the proselytiser, Mort would use social occasions to spread the word of his obsession to New York friends in typically colourful fashion. Dion DiMucci: "Mortie and I hung out together. I used to sit and he'd open a bottle of wine. Mortie would get up in front of us and play Jacques Brel records for us and interpret them. Then he'd play songs from Madrid and interpret them, and German (songs) and interpret them. He spoke eight languages and had a photographic memory. I was in awe, especially listening to him interpret Jacques Brel. He was so flamboyant, he used to have this scarf around his neck and a little glass of wine. He'd be like Laurence Olivier standing up there. It was wonderful."

Performance was the thing for Mort Shuman because it was of the moment. By his own admission he was not a reliable narrator when it came to his own past. In trying to guess how many songs he wrote for Elvis he wrote "sixteen or twenty… it all depends on who's counting and so much for my archives". (The notion of Mort maintaining archives seems in itself amusingly unlikely.) Nor was he much of a strategic planner, more the intuitive gambler. He simply lived for today. It was the source of much of his charm but it did not always pay off. Yet it is impossible to overstate the impact of the modest little off-Broadway Jacques Brel revue he created with Eric Blau – its fifth anniversary warranted an extravaganza performance at Carnegie Hall. In 1973 it was staged in the lobby of Cleveland, Ohio's State Theatre for an intended two-week stint; it was still there in 1975, achieving a 522-performance run that remained one of the longest in the city's history. Yet today the only record we have of anything like the revue in its original form is Denis Héroux's Franco-Canadian film, also dating from 1975, of which *The New York Times* reviewer Vincent Canby wrote: "Mr. Héroux, with the obvious cooperation of Eric Blau and Mort Shuman... has transformed what was essentially a concert into an extravaganza of surreal images that keep messing things up. The images are vivid and disconnected to one another (good) but they inevitably wind up being visual translations of the lyrics (bad)."

Canby's assessment may sound harsh but in retrospect it seems to be an almost generous assessment of an extremely muddled film defeated by its own avant-garde cinematic aspirations that clearly fail to achieve any real equivalence to the original show. Fancy movie effects are everywhere in what still looks like a recorded stage performance even though it was filmed at a movie studio near Nice. It was one of the last films that the Canadian Denis Héroux directed although he continued as a producer for some years. Mort Shuman hated it and all that can be said in its favour now is that at least you get to see Mort enjoying himself, even if, for once, he fails to transmit that enjoyment to anyone else. Also a slightly baffled-looking Jacques Brel puts in an appearance and sings one of his own songs in the alien cinema-scape. The working-class Belgian who once rejected the superficiality of showbiz and lived in near poverty for years to keep singing his raw songs the way he wanted to, had every right to look puzzled by this psychedelic celebration of his life's work. Nonetheless he benefitted from the revue itself which in turn played its part in widening his appeal, prompting very many cover versions of his songs, even though he was far from possessive about them. "He was Flemish," Mort Shuman later recalled, "and you know what the Flemish are like. He didn't care about what we did with his songs. He just wasn't interested."

Scott Walker recorded 'Mathilde', 'Funeral Tango', 'Jacky' and 'My Death'. David Bowie made 'Amsterdam', Dion DiMucci, Dionne Warwick and Johnny Mathis all had versions of 'If We Only Have Love' while Marc Almond recorded 'Jacky'. Many more artists tried English language versions of Brel's visceral and sometimes uncomfortable French-language originals. Perhaps the best memento of the influential Blau-Shuman show is the original cast audio recording where the songs alone tell the story.

When Norman Granz, the influential jazz impresario decided to take the Brel revue to London with its original cast in 1968 the show was a critical success but a commercial flop. It was staged at The Duchess Theatre and lasted for 41 performances. Mort was philosophical. He loved London and for the run of the show could afford to blend it with the hedonist's idea of the best of France by flying to Nice after the last show of the week in the early hours of every Sunday morning, driving to Cannes, checking into a hotel, sleeping for a couple of hours and waking in time for aperitif on The Croisette. Wining, dining and nightclubbing for the rest of the day he would fly back to London on the Monday morning for the first show of the week.

By 1969 Mort had not yet quite cut ties with New York although he no longer wrote with Doc. He produced both words and music for one last Presley offering, 'You'll Think Of Me'. A good song marred by a strange arrangement featuring a faux-sitar sound, it was Mort's second choice, his first being that Kenny Lynch collaboration 'Over My Head'. Even so it was better than Pomus & Shuman's final jointly copyrighted Elvis number, 'Double Trouble', the title song for yet another Presley film that was never in any danger of winning the Palme d'Or at The Cannes Film Festival.

At the same time Mort was recording one of his weirdest hallucinogen-fuelled projects, an album called *My Death*. Something of a song writing *tour de force* it blended many influences and baffled almost all who heard it. It was produced by Jerry Ragovoy, a man who, as Norman Meade, had previously written the odd song with both Doc and Mort as well as some much more famous ones for Irma Thomas and Erma Franklin, respectively 'Time Is On My Side' and 'Piece Of My Heart'. Nothing on My *Death* resembled these songs. Rather it was a Brel-inspired curio that originally came out on Reprise but has since enjoyed re-release on specialist labels. Perhaps its greatest significance to the Mort Shuman story was that it seemed to confirm beyond further question his conversion to adult, earthy music in the Continental tradition while providing a requiem for his New York pop music career. That said it went far beyond the traditional song forms of Brel, as witnessed by its opening track where Mort reads aloud from a medical book a technical text about gynaecology while 'The Hallelujah Chorus' is being performed. One or two Brel songs appear with strange accompaniments, there's a Baudelaire poem (*Les Bijoux*) and Mort's version of another song he wrote with Kenny Lynch and was originally recorded by The Mojos – 'Wait A Minute'. The show-closer, in every sense, is his English-language version of Brel's 'Ma Morte', here presented as an inevitability to be viewed alternately with anxiety and philosophical acceptance: 'But whatever lies behind the door/There is nothing much to do/Angel or devil, I don't care/For in front of that door, there is you'. The song also contains the couplet which could and perhaps should have been his epitaph when Mort's death became a reality 22 years later: 'My death waits to allow my friends/A few good times before it ends'.

From the sublime to the ridiculous in 1970 Mort contributed an original score to a film of truly weird pedigree. *A Day At The Beach* sprang from an idea by Roman Polanski and a novel by Heere Heersma. Polanski co-wrote a screenplay and planned to direct but the notorious murder of his wife by the Charles Manson family forced him to turn the task over to Simon Hesera (a man who, perhaps significantly, was never to direct again except for a documentary about David Ben-Gurion). Peter Sellers has a cameo role as a gay souvenir stall salesman which cannot be classed as one of his subtler performances… which is perhaps which he chose to be credited as 'A. Gay' in the cast list. A rambling and entirely pointless piece about a sociopathic man who takes a little girl (his daughter? Neice?) to a depressingly rainy Danish seaside town while getting progressively more drunk throughout the day, it was allegedly lost for 20 years due to a 'paperwork error' by Paramount Pictures, or perhaps a blessing from some other agency.

Mort Shuman gave the US another try but it no longer matched his increasingly Eurocentric tastes. He never seems to have mentioned it in later years it but early in 1970 Mort is credited with appearing in a short-lived New York run of *Mahagonny,* the first dramatic piece conceived by the partnership of Bertolt Brecht and Kurt Weill. This Brecht-Weill project was manifest in several different formats over a few years, effectively bracketing their more famous *Die Dreigroschenoper* (from which Bobby Darin had famously culled 'Mack The Knife'). It became a scandalous political-satirical opera first performed in Leipzig in 1930. Carmen Capalbo's 1970 off Broadway production at the Phyllis Anderson Theatre marked its first US performance and in it Mort Shuman played alongside Barbara Harris and Estelle Parsons. He seemed to be revisiting musical theatre, perhaps hoping to be involved in something to rival the success of *Jacques Brel Is Alive And Well And Living In Paris*, however *Mahagonny* had a very short run. Certainly mounting a successful musical was something which in later years would come to preoccupy him. When it closed Mort tells of going off to the Greek islands for a summer, on the way back stopping off in Paris where, in his own words, he 'got rid of his American girlfriend' and took a place on the Ile St Louis. "Rock'n'Roll was dead. Long Live Rock'n'Roll" … 'Doc was out of (my) life. (My) contract with the Aberbachs was finished and now (I) would live in Paris." He decided to immerse himself in the culture and pleasures that he loved. It took no time at all. "Gitanes, wine, Left Bank bistros, Right Bank call girls," he recalled without any tinge of regret. "Lots of old and new friends. Gene Kelly couldn't have done it better. Mort was the new American in Paris."

Jacques Brel Is Alive And Well And Living In Paris transferred to its eponymous city, at La Taverne de l'Olympia, a venue not dissimilar to The Village Gate. Mort's new apartment looked out onto The Eiffel Tower and the Champ de Mars, a green park that had once been a military training ground. That apartment would be the launchpad for the new Mort, a man with an astonishing ability to reinvent himself, not in the superficial way of a David Bowie or a Madonna but intrinsically. His facility with languages was one example but even more astonishing was his talent for acquiring new skills, not as a dilettante but as a true enthusiast. His French buddies would be astonished by his wine-tasting skills and all who tasted the elaborate meals he learned to cook were amazed by his culinary talents. One now wonders how he also found time to become an occasional movie actor as well as launching himself as a chart-topping French pop singer.

★   ★   ★

Abraham Lincoln Polonsky had been one of the victims of the Hollywood blacklist in the McCarthy era. Ironically, given his patriotic forenames, he was one of those accused of un-American activities. Before the ban he had directed one of Hollywood's great *films noirs*, *Force Of Evil*, but like others he was reduced to writing screenplays anonymously for a decade, only returning as a director with the well-regarded allegorical Western *Tell Them Willie Boy Is Here* (1969). Exiled in France when he could have been building a career in California, he was a lifelong unrepentant critic of his persecution and forever despised fellow director Elia Kazan who named names at the House Committee on Un-American Activities. Polonsky was appalled when in 1999 the Hollywood Establishment finally gave Kazan a lifetime achievement Oscar, and was unrepentant to be quoted saying he hoped someone would shoot Kazan as it would liven up an otherwise dull evening.

Back in 1971 Polonsky followed up *Tell Them Willie Boy Is Here* with *Romance Of A Horse Thief*, a tale of horse trading in Poland at the time of the Russian-Japanese war of 1904. For this very odd movie Yul Brynner and Eli Wallach were reunited from *The Magnificent Seven*, Serge Gainsbourg and Jane Birkin were reunited from their notoriously explicit 1969 duet 'Je t'aime… Moi Non Plus' (although in real life Gainsbourg rarely let Birkin out of his sight at all). Mort Shuman played a pianist. He also wrote the music for the Yugoslavian-shot film and participated in the shooting, mainly for his own amusement. Since Polonsky's time at New York's City College had been at least 20 years before Mort's, then this was unlikely to have been an 'old school tie' gig, so we must assume that Mort's talent for knowing the right people at the right time was undiminished. In fact Polonsky and Shuman shared a background in that both were the children of Slavic immigrant parents. Louis and Esther Shuman had also suffered from McCarthyism – albeit less catastrophically than Polonsky – in connection with their political activism. So it was that after each daily shoot Shuman, Polonsky and Brynner (born Yuliy Borisovich Bryner in Vladivostok) socialised as a kind of ad hoc East European drinking club. It is hard not to feel that these sessions must have been a great deal more fun than watching the film they made together. *Romance Of A Horse Thief* joins *A Day At The Beach* in the annals of films that may have sounded like a good idea to begin with but were overtaken by circumstances that made them turn out quite otherwise.

On the music front Mort The American In Paris was now in need of a lyricist to match his new musical aspirations. He wanted to break the French market as a mature singer and composer. He discovered that although Jacques Brel was still alive, he was no longer either well or living in Paris, having bought a boat and begun what would become a sporadic series of exotic voyages on which to play out his final days. He would die aged 49 in 1977 of the untreatable lung cancer he had been nursing for some years prior to diagnosis. Brel had already introduced Mort to his manager Charley Marouani who looked after many other big French stars and Marouani had the idea of introducing Mort to Étienne Roda-Gil. It was an inspired decision since Mort, of the photographic memory, was a repository of musical references while Roda-Gil had a kind of literary total recall which enabled him to quote at length and without error from his favourite authors. Again both were the children of émigrés (in Roda-Gil's case Catalans from Spain to France), and the Spanish expatriate had already enjoyed a song writing relationship with the younger Julien Clerc (Paul Alain Leclerc). Shuman and Roda-Gil also shared several other similarities, Mort, until the age of five, speaking only Yiddish in his Brighton Beach *stetl*, Étienne becoming semi-mute until the age of six after being put in the Septandes refugee camp in South West France by his mother immediately after fleeing Spain.

In their respective adolescent years, while Shuman unloaded boxes from ships in New York harbour, Roda-Gil was working in a garage changing oil filters and cleaning whitewall tyres. Blue collar Brooklyn also shared some of the characteristics of Antony, the conurbation where Roda-Gil grew up and which, prior to 1968, was almost a dispossessed province remote from Paris (today it is in the Hauts-de-Seine *departement* in the Île-de-France region). Both men were intelligent, curious about everything, gastronomes and immoderate drinkers.

The differences were significant too. Mort had the talent but not the temperament to be a good student. Étienne always had brilliant scholastic results although later he mocked these as nothing more than evidence of 'arse-licking'. Yet Roda-Gil was a bona fide intellectual who had no hesitation about declaring Mort a quite brilliant man. They would work together and they had an objective. Mort: "What I really wanted to do was create another show like the Brel show, to get more and more into musical theatre. Étienne said well the only way you're going to do it is if you get known, and the way to do that is to make a record." Mort was unsure. He had never made a record apart from demos and sang as part of a troupe on the album from the Jacques Brel show. Roda-Gil was sure he could do it. They decided to create an album together on which Mort would, for the first time, sing in French. It was to be called *Amerika*, the 'k' spelling doubtless a reference to the book by one of Roda-Gil's heroes, Franz Kafka.

Although Roda-Gil the *litterateur* loved several American writers – among them William Faulkner, Erskine Caldwell and John Dos

Passos – he had never set foot in the US. Mort set about putting this right and immediately arranged a trip for him and his wife who was at the time pregnant with their second child, putting them up at the luxurious Plaza Hotel on the south east corner of Central Park. He was their guide in a multi-racial city whose variety of nationalities made a powerful impression on the Roda-Gils. When they too asked him the question that everyone always asked – how many times had he met Elvis Presley – Mort's answer was this time an imaginative one involving Presley's manager, Dutch-born, illegal immigrant, snake-oil salesman and carnival con-man Colonel Tom Parker (Andreas Cornelis van Kuijk). Parker, Mort alleged, said that Presley believed Mort to be a little black kid from Harlem recycling the music of his ancestors. If The King ever found out that Mort was actually a big Jew from Brooklyn that would be the end. No one else has ever advanced this theory, and even Mort's usual line was that since Elvis was forever either cloistered in Memphis or Nashville while Mort was based in New York, the opportunity never arose. His future writing partner Don Black would expand on Mort's attitude saying, "He quite liked never meeting Presley. Basically Mort was a songwriter and he didn't want all that schmoozing and being nice to people, lunches where you've got to be careful what you say. He wasn't that kind of guy anyway." Even so Mort's notion that Parker always contrived to keep his star away from his songwriters was reinforced at a New York press conference in the summer 1972 when Doc Pomus actually got within yards of Presley, only to find his way blocked by Parker who determinedly kept him talking until Presley had disappeared. The relevance of Mort's probably spurious explanation is only that *Amerika* would contain a very good song called 'Black Baudelaire' which suggests that Roda-Gil's poet's imagination may have been fired by the notion of unexpected racial incongruity in the arts.

Now that Roda-Gil had enjoyed a crash course in America spelled with a 'c', all that remained was for Mort to set up a suitably grandiose venue in which they could write the songs for *Amerika* with a 'k'.

"(We) took a monstrous house for the summer to write the songs and have lunches like Eddie Barclay," recalled Mort. "If you happened to drop by at about three pm, on a hot summer afternoon, you'd find everyone asleep, in the bedrooms, on chairs and sofas, on the floor, the grass, all over."

Improbably, in the light of the extravagant diversions Mort arranged for its creation, *Amerika* actually did get written and recorded. It would include a song about Lake Maggiore as well as a paean to an English raincoat and an evocative celebration of the Brighton Beach of Mort Shuman's youth.

The hit single would be the song about the lake, 'Le Lac Majeur'. It is set several thousand miles away from America and seems equally distant from lyrics like 'Each time we have a quarrel, it almost breaks my heart...' It begins:

Il neige sur Le Lac Majeur (It's snowing on Lac Majeur)
Les oiseaux-lyre sont en pleurs (the lyre birds are in tears)
Et le pauvre vin Italien (and the poor Italian wine)
S'est habillé en paille pour rien (is dressed in straw for nothing)

With Mort's soaring melody and vocal and a couple more wintry and opaque verses it became an instant classic. Forty years on they still play it on French radio stations. In later years Mort affably liked to dismiss the lyric: "It's about absolutely nothing. A well-constructed nonsense song but really it's French intellectual rubbish, full of sound and fury and and signifying absolutely bloody nothing. It went gold, so go figure." (The light-hearted disparagement may be because eventually his relationship with Roda-Gil cooled when Mort's new girlfriend first became his lyricist and then his second wife.) Certainly no one could be expected to infer from the song's lyric Roda-Gil's initial germ of inspiration, which, according to Mort, was an anecdote about Mikhaïl Bakounine who allegedly stole the entire proceeds of a party conference in Moscow and took his wife to Lake Maggiore where he staged a grand fireworks display for her benefit, which is what suggested to Roda-Gil the image of snow falling on water. This obscure back story apart, the imagery is really rather effective in its own right as long as you are attuned to expecting poetic lyrics in a popular song… which the French were. The idea of snow falling on a lake, the tear-drop shaped markings on a lyre bird's tail, and the incongruity, in this chilly context, of futile straw summer 'clothing' on a bottle of chianti… all this is surely at least as coherent as many of Bob Dylan's rambling, drug-fuelled songs of the 1960s whose essential meaninglessness left them open to infinite interpretation so garnering admiration for their supposed significance. Seen in this light, Mort's recollections seem uncharacteristically ungenerous towards Roda-Gil. What is more he could sing an elusive lyric like this with enormous passion and enjoyment when he felt like it. There exists a slightly surreal black-and-white video of Mort on some French language TV show playing and singing 'Le Lac Majeur' which, for the occasion, is illogically equipped with its English title ('The Western Shore') and an English lyric. He is singing it as a duet with the Greek vocalist Nana Mouskouri. The key has clearly been selected for her benefit, not his, but to his credit Mort, who may well have had a drink or two, looks entirely at home in this situation, hitting the notes despite the high key and delivering a vigorous and flamboyant piano accompaniment.

It was 1973 and the start of an extraordinary new career for Mort Shuman. At about the same time Pomus biographer Alex Halberstadt claims that back in New York Doc received an unexpected lift when, at a BMI dinner, John Lennon asked to be seated at his table. Lennon was looking tired and harassed as well he might after a period of heavy drinking and the launch of the US Immigration and Naturalization Service's bid to deport him. Even so, it seems they talked all evening, mainly about the past. Yoko Ono was apparently in attendance too, bringing her usual easy charm to the proceedings by slapping away Lennon's hand when he extended it to Doc's companion Shirlee after he had shaken hands with Doc. The story of this encounter may have been exaggerated by Doc himself or by his family and it is hard to verify from any independent sources, but Pomus was just the sort of character John Lennon would admire: a tough, gritty, no-bullshit music business survivor with a chip on his shoulder. Doc certainly kept and displayed a signed photo from Lennon for years afterwards. It is interesting to contrast this meeting with another much shorter one in London at which Ben E. King once introduced Mort Shuman to Paul McCartney at some club. "This is the man who wrote 'Save The Last Dance For Me'," King said by way of introduction. McCartney pumped Mort's hand with the warmth of one tunesmith to another and said, "Great song! Great song!"

9

...and Living in Paris

'Le Lac Majeur' became a hit all over Europe. It is one the best-selling French songs of all-time. Mort recorded it in Italian too, as 'Il Lago Maggiore' and in an English language version for the Anglophone *Amerika* album where it was called 'The Western Shore'. That album was also particularly notable for 'Brooklyn By The Sea', again a Roda-Gil lyric but one informed by Mort's youthful recollections. In its original form the lyric went:

Brooklyn by the sea
Dimanche après-midi (Sunday afternoon)
C'est une vieille promenade (It's an old promenade)
Sur de longues planches maladies (On long, worn planks)
C'est la mer Noire en petit (It's The Black Sea in miniature)
Tout le long de Brighton Beach (All the way along Brighton
    Beach)
A Brooklyn by the sea.

Brooklyn by the sea
Les vieillards assis (The old guys sit)

Se racontent les histoires (Stories are told)

Les défaites et les vieilles gloires (The defeats and the distant
   glories)

Les exodes et les fusils (The retreats and the guns)

Quand ils étaient loin d'ici (When they were far from here…)

De Brooklyn by the sea. (…from Brooklyn by the sea

One of Mort's most evocative performances, 'Brooklyn By The Sea' set the tone for a new chapter in his music. It would often be reflective and romantic, bitter-sweet and thoughtful; Mort was now not out to shock the bourgeoisie any more than he was interested in composing within the narrow parameters of trite teen ballads. After the experimental and (for many) inaccessible *My Death* album, he seemed to have achieved, at a stroke, a more romantic musical appeal that stopped short of being sentimental (even if, in 1974 he did put out an album called *Des Chansons Sentimentales*). The accompanying music videos were quite another story. It has to be said that although Mort's romantic music was often quite sophisticated his French TV appearances where he sang them could make this very easy to forget – a fault of the medium rather than the performer. Aged 35, Mort Shuman was a big, comfortable presence, a *bon viveur* at ease in his new role as a mature singer of grown-up songs. Yet the young radical Mort would have been appalled to see his older self in some of those French television appearances, typically standing at the foot of a flight of stage stairs that led nowhere, looking rather like a geography teacher singing into a hand mike as a worryingly young-looking girl descends in a frilly frock to meet him and be enfolded in his bear-like hug. It was showbiz and Mort went along with it in a country that had inspired him but whose TV, it must be said, has always lagged some considerable distance behind its other media.

He became a star in his own right as well as an enduring fan of jazz, blues, country and the songs of Jacques Brel. Mort continued to ply his trade as a diligent writer and singer who clearly enjoyed fame… indeed it would be difficult to find anyone who enjoyed it more, although occasionally his – what would the adjective be, Brellian? – side came out. Mort's innate distrust of the more superficial trappings of fame and the music business could prompt sudden displays of solidarity with the working class and thinly disguised disdain for the money men. His long-time accountant Aaron Schecter tells of a night in Paris he and his wife spent in the company of Mort as guests at a club called Alcazar where various exotic and unlikely acts performed. Pressed by the club's overweening owner to perform, Mort politely but steadfastly refused. When the man pointed him out to the rest of the audience Mort directed a few amiable words to them but still declined to perform. To the Schecters, who spoke no French, he explained that the owner wanted him to play and sing but he could go and fuck himself. Yet, when the show was over, the diners had all left and the staff were clearing up, Mort had a piano wheeled on and performed for over an hour for the 30-strong assemblage of waiters, bus boys and cleaners who stopped working, sat, listened and applauded. Afterwards he told Schecter that he had played for his 'real public'.

Most of all he enjoyed wining and dining with his buddies, and slipping in and out of affairs and assignations. Johhny Hallyday was one of the entourage. Gérard Baqué was another. Like many young French wannabe rockers, Baqué, a former singer, had grown up listening to Pomus-Shuman, often ambivalently because of the contrast between their cheesy revivals like 'Surrender' (which in fact featured only Doc's lyric and a dutiful demo by Mort) and their great songs like 'Mess Of Blues'. Baqué became, in due course, a fan of Mort the French *chansonnier* but only met him a short while before becoming head of PR for Philips Records. Once installed in that influential job Baqué was summoned by Mort's formidable press officer, Tony Krantz (a woman who represented many French stars including Johnny Hallyday), to advise him of their strategy for Mort's relationship with Philips. Baqué was amused by her assertiveness at what he had assumed was going to be a more equitable discussion but he was nonetheless delighted to be associated with Mort.

In due course Baqué came to marvel at Mort's capacity for the good life, not to mention his appreciation of good food and wine and his newly-acquired prowess as an *haute cuisine* cook. (Was any *arriviste* American in Paris ever greeted with such wonderment as Mort, a benign invader who seemed intent upon outdoing the French at their own national obsessions with wine and food?)

"When there were ten guests, he would cook for twenty," Baqué recalled. "Johnny (Hallyday) ... and so many others remember his 'Jambalaya' or his scallops in a wine jelly. The wine – Pommard and Pauillac, Sauternes or Saumur? He knew them all! Triumphant in blind tastings, (he had) the most refined taste buds."

The year after *Amerika* was released Mort's second album of collaboration with Roda-Gil, *Voilà Comment*, came out. This time Roda-Gil's literary influence showed through in strange titles like *Noces de Carabosse et de Nosferatu* (evoking the imaginary nuptials of the Wicked Fairy of the Sleeping Beauty legend and the Dracula-like monster of Murnau's famous German Expressionist horror film). It was not an obvious crowd-pleaser. In 1974, *Des Chansons Sentimentales* was released but met with less success than its predecessors. Mort then wrote the original music for *Les Guichets du Louvre*, the first film to be made about a dark episode of World War II when the French police rounded up Jews in a Paris velodrome preparatory to sending them off to the Nazi camps. It was a deplorable act of complicity with the German occupiers that shocks each subsequent French generation anew when they find out about it. Joseph Losey would also tackle the subject in *Mr Klein* and Gilles Paquet-Brenner made it central to the harrowing *Sarah's Key* (*Elle s'appelait Sarah*) in 2010. *Les Guichets du Louvre* was by far the most serious film that Mort Shuman ever became involved with and we can only speculate to what extent he undertook it thinking of the lost family members Louis Schulman left behind in Poland.

In the summer of 1974 Mort was briefly reunited with a member of another family from his past, Doc and Willi's daughter Sharon. Now 16 and affecting a new spelling of her given name, Sharyn was sent to France on the initiative of her grandmother Millie who wanted to get her out of Doc's smoky apartment where she had moved after relations with Willi had deteriorated. Something cultural was intended – she was visiting France to study art – and, once Doc had tracked down Mort's whereabouts, Sharyn stayed briefly with him in one of his summer retreats. (It was on this trip that Sharyn would also meet her future husband Will Bratton, who was renovating the former summer home of Simone DeBeauvoir which was about to become American art school.) Chez Mort, Sharyn was confronted with quite a transformation. Sun-tanned, wealthy and adored, Mort was living a life that could not have been more different from that of her father who was definitely not doing well. We can only speculate whether this conspicuous contrast in fortunes made a lasting impression on the young Sharyn Felder who in later life has always sought to downplay Mort Shuman's significance in her father's professional life. Doc was now living in a small and increasingly cramped apartment with Shirlee Hauser and Sharyn too ever since she had fallen out with her mother. The old crowd was disappearing. Paul Case died. J. Leslie McFarland also passed away, dying of exposure after falling asleep drunk in a freezing tenement basement. Doc was scraping a living hosting and playing poker games. As if in a spirit of sympathy, only the year before The Broadway Central had chosen to give up the ghost and partially collapsed in a cloud of dust, killing four residents.

In 1975 the US Columbia label reissued the *Jacques Brel Is Alive...* album and meanwhile Mort, recently infatuated by, and now married to Élisabeth Moreau, collaborated with the new woman in his life on most of the songs that would appear on the 1976 album *Imagine...*

The album's big hit song would be 'Papa-Tango-Charly', co-written not with Moreau but with Philippe Adler who was later aggrieved to find that the other songs he had co-written for the album with Mort had subsequently been entrusted to Moreau who had modified his words, appended her name and subsequently benefitted disproportionately from the album sales. "What's more she never dreamed of thanking me for letting her hitch a ride on my wagons," Adler later complained. Mort had initially seen Adler as a successor to Roda-Gil who in turn felt that Moreau had contributed to the erosion of his working relationship with Mort. Roda-Gil said of her, with his poet's fondness for ellipsis: "Tous les mirages qui coûtent cher font rêver" (loosely: "all our most painful illusions help us to dream"). Hardly much clearer than his elusive lyrics for 'Le Lac Majeur' Roda-Gil's verdict does nonetheless imply that he always saw the Shuman/Moreau marriage as being made somewhere other than in heaven.

It also, strangely, prefigures what Mort would write in 1991 about loving Hamburg despite having such painful memories of an affair there: "Things you love the most, sometimes evolve from unhappy, desperate experiences." In 1975 the union had produced Mort's first daughter, Barbara, and her birth was evoked in the title track of *Imagine...* which was why, of this collection, it was that song which held the most significance for him. Despite the massive success of 'Papa-Tango-Charly' the Shuman/Adler collaboration never really got into gear mainly because Adler was temperamentally unsuited to joining Mort's band of good-time buddies quite apart from self-confessedly being financially unable to keep up with them. Together they wrote a critically acclaimed song for the well-known Régine (Regina Zylberberg) called 'L'Emmerdeuse' ('The Troublemaker') but the record never sold. Even so Adler's personal recollections of Mort remained exclusively warm. One lingering disappointment was that he believed that 'Papa-Tango-Charly' could have been an international hit because his original lyric contained phrases that were understood in many countries, added to which Mort wrote an English lyric for it too which Adler felt completely respected the original lyric structure. That it never became a global hit remained "one of the regrets of my life," Adler said, "but in the end my biggest regret is that Mort had to pass away so soon."

The next film Mort composed for was considerably lighter in tone than *Les Guichets du Louvre*. *A Nous Les Petites Anglaises!* (*Let's Get Those English Girls!*) was a playful piece about some French boys who fail their English exam and are sent to England instead of the Côte d'Azur which they had been promised had they passed. Directed by Michel Lang and set in the English seaside town of Ramsgate (which you have to have visited to appreciate the comic contrast with the Côte d'Azur), the film was both a commercial and a personal success for Mort Shuman, featuring one of his biggest French hits 'Sorrow'. It must have been a busy time for him as he scored three more French movies released in 1976 and, more interestingly, acted in a hypnotically strange French-Canadian film that fully deserves its cult status if only for its casting.

The Little Girl Who Lives Down The Lane was one the first films made by Jodie Foster (Alicia Christian Foster) after her controversial appearance as Iris Steensma, the 12-year-old prostitute in Martin Scorsese's *Taxi Driver*. This time she was teamed with Alexis Smith (Gladys Smith) who had been a Hollywood star in the 1940s and 1950s but by the 1970s was a gracefully ageing TV actress back in her native Canada. Also starring was Martin Sheen (Ramon Estevez) not yet a big star but already on his way up after his memorable turn in Terrence Malick's film *Badlands*. Completing the quartet of leading players was Mort Shuman who was originally approached to write the film's music but instead ended up playing a cop called Miglioriti. Without question he gives the best performance of anyone in this contrived thriller which is allegedly based on a novel by Laird Koenig but clearly owes more to Koenig's own adaptation of his book for the theatre. Housebound and stagy *The Little Girl Who Lives Down The Lane* is really very odd indeed but Shuman's acting is naturalistic and pitch-perfect throughout, especially in his scenes with Foster. Director Nicolas Gessner said that found Mort a quick study, adding that he thought singers often made good dramatic actors because they were used to pushing their performances to the limit. It sounds like a dubious assertion (as anyone who has seen Barbra Streisand or Liza Minnelli acting at their least restrained might attest) but as it happened it was true in Mort's case; Mort and Jodie Foster did indeed get on well and Gessner recognised that their affinity transmitted itself to their performances. There exist some informal snapshots of Mort and Jodie clowning in front of the Eiffel tower, blowing out candles on a birthday cake and of her standing behind him as he plays piano. They shared an affinity for the French language too; the future star of *The Accused* and *Silence Of The Lambs* attended the French-language Lycée Français de Los Angeles, making her one of the few Hollywood actors able to dub her own voice for the Francophone movie market. She even appears in a small French-speaking part in Jean-Pierre Jeunet's 2004 tour de force *Un Long Dimanche de Fiançailles* (*A Very Long Engagement*).

It is a matter of considerable regret that *Rue Haute* (*High Street*) (1976), directed by André Ernotte, has disappeared from view since the few who ever saw it consider it to be a fine film. Set in Brussels and based on novel by Ernotte's partner Elliot Tiber (Elliot Teichberg) it starred Belgian actress Annie Cordy (Léonie Cooreman) as Mimi, a mentally disturbed woman, and Mort Shuman as David Reinhardt, an American artist who is drawn into tracing the roots of Mimi's condition back to her experiences in WW2.

Mort's original film music of 1976 saw him working on three erotic films. He wrote the score for *Une Femme Fidèle*, directed by soft porn specialist Roger Vadim as a loose remake of *Dangerous Liaisons* and starring Sylvia Kristel of *Emmanuelle* fame. He shared music credits with Christian Gaubert (who in the end scored *The Little Girl Who Lives Down The Lane*) for François Reichenbach's documentary *Sex O'Clock USA*. Finally he teamed up with the now-notorious Catherine Breillat (dubbed 'porno auteuriste' by some for her sexually explicit films like *Romance* [1999] and *À Ma Soeur!* [2001]). Mort scored Breillat's very first film *Une Vraie Jeune Fille* which set the tone for her career by featuring the sexual self-exploration of a 14-year-old girl filmed in sometimes gynaecological close up. Mort is credited as 'Schuman' not Shuman for unclear reasons. He is also credited with co-authoring three of the film's songs with Breillat who, having based her own screenplay on her own novel and directed the film as

114

well as being its production designer was obviously in no way shy about becoming Mort's song writing partner *du jour*.

Around 1976 Mort met the woman who would eventually become his third wife, Maria-Pia Vezia. Her response to Mort's still ebullient lifestyle of excess was characterised by Gérard Baqué, one of his regular hell-raising friends, as a model of tolerance. "The beautiful and sweet Maria-Pia who knew her husband Mortimer better than anyone dreaded our evenings out but also welcomed us with a smile," he wrote. "Generous and lucid, there was never cynicism, immodesty or despair in Mort's house."

In fact Mort did not become Maria-Pia's husband until Easter of 1979 when in what she now makes sound like a spontaneous decision after three years of doubts on her part, they married in Florida where they were visiting Mort's mother, now conventionally retired in The Sunshine State. "We never celebrated our wedding anniversary so I would have to look up the date!" she adds but, with so many ambiguous dates dotted throughout the almanac of the Pomus-Shuman story, one more makes little difference and there seems no reason to put her to the trouble. Mort was already father to Barbara from his second marriage and Maria-Pia would give him two more. She was already part of his life in Paris and would become ever more important to him during the final years in that city and the start of a new life London. She was also one of the few people to be privy to Mort's day-to-day method of working.

"Mainly I would say he had his music in his head," she explains. "I can give you an example. He would always come with me if I went shopping or wanted to buy a new pair of shoes and if there was music in the shop he'd say, oh I'll wait for you outside because I have something in mind and I don't want to lose it. Then one day he would sit and the piano and produce the song which he had kept in his head. He would work when he had to in the sense that he was always happy and wanting to work... but he had so many other things that interested him. He loved cooking, having his friends around. He would fit his work and his interests together as well as he could… and he managed pretty well!"

In 1977 Mort worked with Michel Lang again, this time on another seaside film *L'Hôtel De La Plage* set in Brittany during the August holiday season. The film's setting and structure are reminiscent of Jacques Tati's *Les Vacances de M. Hulot* (1953) and it was to Lang's credit that his gentle amusement focusing on middle-age infidelities and teenage romances managed to avoid invidious comparisons with Tati's sublime and almost wordless comedy. The soundtrack album brought together a number of Mort's French colleagues and friends featuring tracks by Eddy Mitchell, Richard Anthony and Hugues Aufray. It also introduced Mort's romantic *Un Été de Porcelaine*, one of his most memorable French hits whose dreamy charm even a reliably bad music video could not harm. Altogether Mort Shuman wrote music for fifteen films during his Paris period. Some of these are now rather obscure and several had strictly French appeal in the first place. Cataloguing them all in detail might prove tiresome for the non-French reader so I have concentrated on the better known examples or those that illustrate something of Mort's particular talent or his enduring facility for working with interesting creative colleagues.

Those 15 do not include the additional movies where he is credited with having written or co-written a song or songs featured in films. That process had begun with the 1962 low-budget Milton Subotsky-produced, Richard Lester-directed pop film *It's Trad Dad* (*Ring-A-Ding Rhythm* in the US) which contained some traditional jazz (prompted by an essentially British revival of the music at the time) but also featured the Pomus-Shuman hits 'Seven Day Weekend', and 'You Never Talked About Me' and the Shuman-Lynch-Westlake song 'What Am I To You?'. American performers Del Shannon, Gary 'US' Bonds, Chubby Checker and Gene McDaniels were also slotted into what passes for a plot, no doubt in the hope of boosting the movie's US chances, though with little success. It was a cheap and dislocated looking film and at the time it was hard to envisage its ex-patriate director (Richard Lester from

116

Philadelphia) going on to greater things. He did: The Beatles' two movies, *The Knack… And How To Get It*, *How I Won The War*, *Petulia*, two films in the Superman franchise and the enchantingly mock-heroic and bitter-sweet *Robin And Marian* were just a few of the films that would be racked up by this influential and most personable of directors.

At least a couple of dozen other films, quite apart from the Presley movies, featured a song or songs co-written by Mort Shuman and the tally continues to grow today since some of those peppy Brill Building ditties gradually became pop standards. Added to this Mort's songs – most regularly those composed with Doc – have been used in many international TV programmes and series ranging from *The Muppet Show* to *The Sopranos*.

There were other albums, including *My Name Is Mortimer* (1977) and, revisiting one of the literary images of his life, the album *Le Nègre Blanc* (1978) which apart from the title track did little to reflect the cultural convulsions that had prompted Norman Mailer's original coinage. The French public was not tiring of the tireless Mort Shuman, yet still he was not fulfilled. What he really wanted to do was to build on the stage success of *Jacques Brel Is Alive And Well And Living In Paris*. His 1983 bid to achieve this was the proposed show *Ma Ville*, effectively a love letter to Paris which he created with Loïc Le Guen and Claude Lemesle. The album eventually appeared but the show was never performed, despite much lobbying of the Paris Town Hall. Lacking a theatrical run to tie the songs together, the unperformed *Ma Ville* project remained a source of bitter disappointment to its creator who perhaps felt that he had been spurned by the object of his affection. Still, his ambition to mount a successful musical did not subside, even though his next bid would be in a different capital city.

★ ★ ★

In the aftermath of the *Ma Ville* disappointment Mort travelled to Nashville, Tennessee, to accept a BMI Award for Dolly Parton's 1984

Top 5 Country hit of 'Save The Last Dance For Me', a record whose royalties garnered both Doc and Mort more than the rest of their combined earnings for that year. Doc was in Nashville too, despite his dislike of travelling and his distaste for country music. Doc and companion Shirlee Hauser were in fact installed in the hotel room adjacent to Mort's, proof that even staid organisations like Broadcast Music, Inc. are capable of the odd playful gesture since they had made the bookings. Mort and Doc had not met for years. Shirlee had technically moved out of Doc's apartment, but only to a higher floor of the same building which meant they still spent a lot of time together. His poker playing circuit had started to invite the attentions of criminals and after a robbery perpetrated by crooks disguised as cops, Doc once again started to sense the end of an era without having much idea about what would replace it. He had become one of the faces around the music clubs, a living institution, a reminder of past glories, a dependably salty analyst of the infinitely devious world of the music business, and a man who characteristically began any anecdote or diatribe with the phrase "D'ya believe this shit?" Still a dyed-in-the-wool blues fanatic, he would occasionally canvass on behalf of one his favourite performers, including the serially unsuccessful Little Jimmy Scott who was still plying his trade to dwindling audiences. He wrote the odd song with a variety of collaborators but none had really gelled. More recently Doc had tried writing with two drug addicts who, mainly due to their habit, sometimes made the old, feckless Mort look almost dependable: Willy De Ville (William Paul Borsey Jr.) late of Mink DeVille, and Malcolm John 'Mac' Rebennack, Jr., aka Doctor John. Despite the difficulties these had been more promising alliances.

In Nashville Doc and Mort talked into the night with genuine affection, making optimistic plans for a reunion. There is a picture of them together showing Mort in a Stetson and tuxedo with his arm draped around Doc's shoulders. After the awards Mort went back to New York for a spell, ostensibly to write with Doc. The country music theme persisted. Doc and Mort went to what was once a famous Texas outpost a stone's throw from New York's Washington Square. For those who never saw it, one of the more arresting sights on lower Fifth Avenue between 1976 and 1989 was The Lone Star Café, previously a branch of Schrafft's restaurant chain which in its new guise was adorned with a large replica of an iguana on the roof of its entrance. Texas country music was The Lone Star Café's staple although the venue attracted a wide range of other music acts to play in front of its cramped bar where you could sit with your beer and almost be onstage with the band whether you wanted to be or not. When Doc and Mort paid their nostalgic visit in 1984 The Drifters, interpreters of some of the best Pomus-Shuman hits, were onstage and Josh Alan Friedman later wrote of that evening:

"(Doc and Mort's) chemistry electrified The Lone Star where Charlie Thomas and The Drifters kept an onstage patter going toward them. Mort heckled like a banshee, belting out bold new harmonies to 'Hushabye', 'I Count The Tears' and other Drifters songs he'd co-written. Doc rolled his eyes, ever the straight man, but seemed humbled by this lusty animal, Mort Shuman, who had been his partner in so much glory."

In New York Doc and Mort duly started writing a country-flavoured song together but it was never completed, and, predictably, Mort soon drifted back to France. Jerome Felder and Mortimer Shuman would never see one another again.

★   ★   ★

Back in Paris Mort came up with a concept album called *Pharoan* co-written with Julien Sednal and which, despite finding favour with traditional radio broadcasters, came at exactly the wrong time for the sudden influx of independent FM stations who were disinclined to play this unclassifiable melange of *chanson* and rock with its abrupt shifts of mood and subject matter. Even so, Yves Mourousi, one of France's most influential television and radio news presenters and journalists of the time, opened up The Louvre Museum to shoot a memorable music video for the single 'Pharoan'. Mourousi also co-wrote 'ÇaVa...' with Mort, a huge disco single with another impressive setting for its music video: The Palais des Congrès.

The comparative failure of the *Pharoan* album was another cause of regret to Mort who in 1986 threw himself into a potentially exciting new project: the offer to co-star in a film provisionally entitled *La Jonque* (meaning 'The Junk' in the sense of Chinese boat) to be directed by Claude Bernard-Auber. Its big appeal was that Mort's co-star would be Lino Ventura (Angiolino Ventura), for 30 years a huge film star in France which claimed him as its own even though he never gave up his Italian citizenship. Eventually the film became a victim of 'production hell', the notoriously treacherous terrain stretching between concept and shooting. When Mort met with Ventura for lunch in connection with the project he brought along drinking buddy Gérard Baqué who later pointed out that he had noticed that for the first time no one in the restaurant had pestered Mort for an autograph. "Yes," Mort agreed afterwards, "because it's the first time you've had lunch with a real star – Lino. No one dares to trouble the stars." Setting up the movie dragged on and on and then Ventura suddenly died of a heart attack.

Nearing the end of his 13-year French sojourn Mort wrote another original film score, this time for Jacques Richard's pre-Euro film *Cent Francs L'Amour* a forgettable drama about a peep-show whose entrance fee is the 100 francs of the title and where love threatens to bloom between art photographer Jeremy and peep-show performer Otie. Mort sang two of the songs he wrote for the picture.

Then The Shumans relocated to London, *en famille*. It was late 1986. Why leave Paris, which had been so good to Mort?

"I'd become like a decaying MOR star over there," he later recalled candidly. He had always liked London and seemed curiously indifferent to New York. As a place to be born he simply said that New York "could have been worse" but it seemed that somehow Europe always made a better playground for his sensibilities. On settling in London his first major project would be another bid to write a musical, perhaps in part to exorcise the lingering disappointment with *Ma Ville…* but then again, perhaps not – Mort was not one to dwell on the past, whether it was a time of success or failure. On the other hand he liked nothing more than pleasing the crowd as long as the work was good, but he could not fail to be aware that his income continued to derive mainly from 20-year-old successes and not more recent ones. He harboured a wish to create a musical based on Vittorio de Sica's 1948 film *Ladri di biciclette (Bicycle Thieves)*. As it turned out his next opportunity to tackle a big stage musical would owe less to Italian neo-realistic cinema than to the diluted legacy of social-realism in the British novel, a movement that had begun in the 1950s and flourished in the 1960s. Although much lighter *Budgie*: *The Musical* would owe something to the gritty tradition of the novels *Saturday Night And Sunday Morning*, *The Loneliness Of The Long Distance Runner* and *Billy Liar,* all of which were subsequently filmed. This last had been a bleak but touching novel (then a play and then a film) centring on a Walter Mitty-ish Yorkshire lad whose fantasies at first shielded him from drab routines of working-class life and then robbed him of the courage to escape from them. It had successfully been turned into a musical with Michael Crawford and Elaine Paige taking the leads, music by John Barry and lyrics by Don Black. Its success suggested the idea of creating another a musical about a lovable loser, this time based not on a novel but on a TV series that had already proved a successful vehicle for former pop idol Adam Faith (Terence Nelhams) in the early 1970s. Black was slated to write the lyrics, with Keith Waterhouse & Willis Hall to write the show's book. All they needed now was someone to write the music.

10

London Calling

So again, why London? Maria-Pia Shuman confirms that departure from France was inevitable and that there were good reasons for selecting London.

"Mort wanted to be the Offenbach of the 20th century," she says, "and in France he had simply done all that he could do. He had been a writer, performer, artist, film actor and composer of music for films. Now what he wanted was to write for theatre. He wanted to create a musical. He had written that most beautiful *hommage* to Paris called *Ma Ville* working with Claude Lemesle. It really was the most extraordinary work and they tried for two years to put it on. It was a big show, a big production and there was always a problem – no theatre or problems with a director. Writing it had taken maybe 18 months then he spent another two years knocking on every single door… and remember he was very popular, everybody liked him so much and no one had doubts about the quality of his music. Still, it never came together. They were always waiting for someone or something. The album came out but it was not really a success on its own. That, I can assure you, was the end of France for Mort Shuman! He said 'Everything I could do in France I did. Now, goodbye'."

Maria-Pia, who could not remember offhand the date of their marriage, instantly remembered that it was February 6, 1986 that they moved to London. It sounded like a happy moment.

"Mortie always liked the British people and London in particular," she says. "What he liked was that people in Britain always knew about his music and his American past. The French didn't. Here he wouldn't need to explain who he was and what he had done. He liked the style of living and he liked the music scene. What he wanted to do was to write music for the stage, he wanted to do musicals and the place to do it was London."

Asked whether the contrast in cuisine might have come as something of a shock she replies rather diplomatically that while Mort had certainly embraced the heady wining and dining aspect of Paris, "we were fortunate enough to arrive in London in the mid-eighties when already the culinary experience was really changing a lot".

There is no question that London was a good fit for Mort at this particular time. He acquired a British manager, Charles Negus-Fancey who still looks after Mort's legacy and his family's interests. Mort now wanted to pursue his ambitions to create a musical out of *Bicycle Thieves* by involving British stage director Mike Ockrent. However even discussing it seriously had to wait because in 1986 Ockrent – who had made a career in London directing small, intimate plays as well as some more extravagant productions – was busy transferring *Me And My Girl* from London to Broadway. So the project which instead presented itself to Mort was *Budgie*, the proposed Adam Faith musical which had the unusual advantage of being able to use the same actor who had originally made the title role famous in straight drama because Faith himself had started out as a pop singer. A good-looking boy with an unremarkable yet tuneful voice, Faith had matured into a decent actor and a thoughtful man with some sense of realism about the opportunities open to old rock'n'rollers. The future lyricist of *Budgie* was Don Black (Donald Blackstone) who, by 1986, had already made a major name for himself as the lyricist for several James Bond movie songs,

'Born Free', 'To Sir, With Love' and the 1979 song cycle *Tell Me On A Sunday* with Andrew Lloyd Webber, not to mention the songs for *Billy* (the *Billy Liar* musical) written with John Barry. Mort's publisher suggested that Don should meet Mort Shuman so launching a memorable friendship that today Don Black still talks about with immense affection.

"First of all, it's not too strong to say I loved him," he says. "Mort was the most lovable man, irresistible. I'll never forget the first time I met him. His publisher had said you'd really get on well with him. I was living in Basil Street in Knightsbridge and so we met at the (nearby) Capital Hotel. Mort got hold of me, hugged me – almost crushed me, he was that sort of guy – and said, 'This is a celebration – Shuman and Black together! Let's have a drink!' There was a bar there and, well, I'm not a very big drinker and I've never felt so silly. I think ordered a Cinzano Bianco or something like that and he ordered two bottles of Chardonnay. Of course I ended up drunk and he was marvellous – a joy to be with. We ended up writing the *Budgie* musical together but the real joy was in his friendship. All my sisters fell in love with him, he was part of the family. For that matter writing *Budgie* was a joy too because he was such a great talent and, oh, he wanted to write 20 musicals with me! We even started another one, *The Legend Of Johnny Appleseed* and we got as far as writing a couple of very funny songs for that."

Budgie finally hit the boards in 1988, opening at the Cambridge Theatre in London. Don Black suggests that putting it together had been such fun that it was almost reward enough in itself and Mort Shuman's infectious enthusiasm was to a large extent responsible for that. Co-starring with Adam Faith was Anita Dobson who had just finished a memorable three-year stint as Angie Watts in the BBC soap opera *EastEnders* and would soon marry astrophysicist and Queen guitarist Brian May. The show itself is worth considering in some detail if only because of Mort's imaginative music. According to Don Black, Mort believed one of its songs, 'In One Of My Weaker Moments' was among the best he had composed. Don Black still professes his own particular affection for another song 'If It Wasn't For The Side Effects'. Keith Waterhouse and Willis Hall's book for the show was an ebullient but rather densely plotted tale set in Soho's sleazy world of strip-clubs, sex-shops and porno bookstores. Budgie Bird, small-time thief and would-be con-man, is employed by the local porn-king, Charlie Endell, to lure punters into the Naughty Nighties strip-club. A psychopathic villain on the run seeks refuge inside the strip-club and just before his arrest hands over a brief-case full of cash to Budgie who hides it in the club. The stage is set, literally, for the conflicting desires of Budgie's penniless live-in girlfriend (Hazel), Budgie's own gambling urges and a subsidiary plot about a stripper's baby being offered to the local bookmaker whose young wife has just lost her own child at birth. There is a good strand focussing on the kind of Italian restaurant that helped to define the ambiance of Soho in those days but in the end Budgie Bird remains a loser who just about gets by on charm while Hazel exudes the hopeless hopefulness of the serial emotional victim perennially defeated by her own good nature.

In a 'what-if' sort of way it is interesting to contrast *Budgie*'s very busy ducking-and-diving plot with the stark and spare storyline of *Bicycle Thieves*, the film which Mort longed to turn into a musical. All that happens in de Sica's beautiful but profoundly depressing movie is that a poverty-stricken man in post-war Rome has the bicycle stolen that is crucial to his hard-won new job and represents his only hope for his family's future. He and his little boy search for it for two days and fail to find it. In utter desperation the man tries to steal a replacement but is immediately caught and only saved from being turned over to the police out of disdainful pity from the crowd that has captured him. His son has seen him humiliated. He has lost his job and his self-respect. *FINE*.

As for *Budgie* the Black/Shuman pairing did manage to match Mort's clever melodies with Don's salty and plausible London speech. It must have looked like Mort Shuman had found a happy successor to his early French lyric writers who made the local words to his universal music sound instantly authentic for native audiences. In retrospect perhaps this particular musical came a little too late for British public taste. After all *Budgie* had already been a hit TV series a decade before and another TV series, *Minder,* had mined similar territory more successfully and with occasional flashes of genuine comic brilliance. Perhaps the lovable London rogue formula, even as a musical, was slightly passé in the affluent late 1980s; ironically even the real Soho, a stone's throw from the Cambridge Theatre, was itself showing early if patchy signs of gentrification. In any event *Budgie* closed after three months, losing money and still not providing Mort with a new hit musical show.

"It's funny," Don Black suggests, "that when a show doesn't work people do tend to exaggerate and say, oh it was complete disaster. The other day I was on TV talking about musicals and I mentioned how people say that *Sunset Boulevard* – which ran for three and a half years – and *Aspects of Love* – which ran for four years – did not do well! But I think that's because Andrew Lloyd Webber had things that run for 20 years! Some people loved *Budgie* – Mark Steyn for example wrote a review of that in which he said he thought it was one of the great musicals of all time. Mort and I spent hours afterwards wondering why the hell didn't it work and we came to the conclusion that while we had been hoping for an English version of *Guys And Dolls* perhaps people simply didn't want to spend an evening with a lot of tarts and layabouts. My lasting memory of *Budgie* is just sitting round with Mort on piano having fun. Certainly his music was very much attuned to the story. It had a jagged edge – moody when it had to be, heart-breaking for some of the tarts' songs... look, Mort could do anything musically. I think he liked working with me because he liked the discipline of the rhymes. He could write for Elvis Presley and The Drifters and there's a kind of looseness to that, a kind of streetwise shrug. But when you write for musicals it calls for a different kind of music."

Despite the slightly rueful aftermath of *Budgie*'s three-month run, Mort's life was fuller than ever on every front. Maria-Pia Shuman had given birth to two daughters, Maria-Pia and Eva-Maria, step-sisters for Barbara. In 1989 he embarked on writing another musical project, this time with Ray Connolly, to be entitled *Save The Last Dance For Me*. Unlike the musical show of the same name which made its debut in 2012, this earlier venture was intended to incorporate many of Pomus-Shuman's most familiar songs and add some new ones by Mort to the framework of a gritty story set in a multi-racial Lower East Side New York neighbourhood at the time of the Cuban missile crisis. Connolly, the Lancashire-born novelist, screenwriter and journalist, had grown up loving Pomus-Shuman songs and had first met Mort in the early 1970s. By the late 1980s, now with well-regarded screenplays for the films *That'll Be The Day* and *Stardust Memories* under his belt as well as a number of TV plays and novels, he was re-introduced to Mort and with the encouragement of producer Chris Malcolm, started work on the new project. Even though this particular *Save The Last Dance For Me* would never make it to the stage, the Shuman/Connolly collaboration revealed Mort working with apparently undiminished vigour despite some signs of failing health evidenced by his giving up alcohol (Don Black recalls Mort selecting fine wines and saying, "I can't drink it – enjoy it for me"). For Ray Connolly, an unashamed fan, it was a deeply satisfying experience to work with someone who had first touched his life when he had been an impressionable adolescent noting with wonder the mysterious 'Pomus-Shuman' credit on *both* sides of his copy of '(Marie's The Name) His Latest Flame'/'Little Sister'.

"I was very keen on who wrote what," he recalls, "and I went back and looked at some other records to see what else they had written." Like all true fans he does not hesitate when asked if he can name his favourite among their compositions. "Yes! 'Doin' The Best I Can'," he says. "It's such a sad song, this guy saying I'm doing the best I can and the girl saying it's not enough." The song was rather thrown away in the Elvis movie *GI Blues* as a romantic number performed live in a bar and cut short by a fight, so 'Doin' The Best

I Can' was easy to overlook at the time and yet it features one of Mort's most lovely, soaring melodies. Elvis chose to perform it doing his Ink Spots' impersonation (also to be heard on a better-known earlier track, his version of 'That's When Your Heartaches Begin').

"I remember saying to Mortie that it was one of their greatest songs," says Ray Connolly, "and he said, mmm, I don't think so… and I said, I'm telling you Mortie, *it is!*" On another occasion Mort said of the song, "Doc and I were into Don Robertson who was a great country and western writer, his songs were just spot-on, like 'I Really Don't Want To Know'. We were in that Don Robertson, easy country, ballady mood, and that is how it came out."

As ever, Mort Shuman wrote, played and sang with prodigious facility when working with Connolly. "What happened was we had all the hit songs and I would say we need a new song here, a sad song. And the next day he'd turn up with one. Then I'd say, 'Play "Mess Of Blues",' and he'd play it but not the way it was recorded. He'd change the tune and do another version of it… which would have been equally great."

Connolly also recalls a song written for a different project. "I'd written a TV series called *Perfect Scoundrels* and I wanted a country and western-type song. I said it's called *Blue Kisses* Morty. He got down to work straight away and came back with it the next day. He played it and the piano sound was slightly jazzy. I said, 'No, I want a Floyd Cramer sound', and he said, 'Oh like this?' And of course he could play it that way too."

As for their ill-fated musical, it was more or less completed but Connolly acknowledges now that his fear-of-nuclear-Armageddon idea was too dark. "It was just the wrong show for the wrong time," he says. Then a publisher's offer of a two-book deal finally meant he had to stop working on the final stages of *Save The Last Dance For Me* and turn his attention to writing something that would earn him money. The project went off the boil and even later any lingering hopes of one day reviving the show disappeared after the bombing of The World Trade Center, an event whose hideous reality banished forever the prospect of a popular musical based on New Yorkers' fears of mass destruction.

★   ★   ★

Mort and Doc's final meeting had been back in 1984, the same year Millie Felder died aged 83, surviving her husband Morris by six years even though his final two decades had been spent in a home suffering from dementia. Shirlee Hauser, Doc's long time platonic companion, finally got married and was now Shirlee Friedman; her husband Howard must have been very understanding because Doc found it hard to let go and she was inclined to indulge him. In 1977 Doc produced an album for Roomful Of Blues as well as the first sessions for the Austin group, The Fabulous Thunderbirds. Although Doc always listed his number in the telephone directory he pretended to resent being sent tapes after *Rolling Stone* magazine called him a talent scout, claiming that he didn't like getting unsolicited tapes as "I might steal something subconsciously". His grown-up children Sharyn and Geoffrey would come and see him. So would his brother Raoul and wife Myrna. In time even Shirlee would visit with her son whose middle name – Jeromy – was not a spelling mistake but a gracious nod towards Doc's given name.

Doc kept up his gregarious lifestyle, newly determined to be a living legend, not a forgotten one, ever since that meeting with Lennon, an event that was immortalised in a photograph of them together that Doc kept at home. He was still playing the 'no bullshit, tell it like it is' old sage, still attracting the attentions of the great and the good and occasionally still dazzling impressionable young women. In 1986 Bob Dylan had paid Doc a visit at The Westover Hotel, leaving behind the vague suggestion that they might even write together although this never came to anything. (Dylan did however contribute a track to the 'tribute' album *Till The Night Is Gone* – Doc's old number for Big Joe Turner 'Boogie Woogie Country Girl'). Later, at Doc's apartment there would be occasional

130

visits from Tom Waits, Lou Reed, Marshall Crenshaw and Dr. John who would dispense their wisdom at an informal workshop that Doc had started hosting for 20 or so would-be song writers, each of whom was given a weekly assignment like a love song or a novelty song, which were then critiqued by the class. Carole King dropped in. The young Shawn Colvin found Doc's advice abrasive but useful. Even so, mixed messages were not unknown; Doc liked to put down his own work when it suited him saying things like, "The roots of pop music should be classical, jazz, blues and evergreen pop writers like Irving Berlin and George Gershwin, not rock'n'roll writers like Chuck Berry and even myself. That is why the current music scene is so silly and meaningless and second rate."

Lou Reed offered some song writing advice of his own to Doc which may have been less than welcome: don't repeat verses. Doc's reply was that he was just an old blues writer, an honest enough admission although like many people, Doc was not above re-inventing the past to suit the present. He had once dismissed newcomer Bob Dylan's 'fuck-everything' approach. He had been unimpressed by The Beatles when their rise threatened the ruling Brill Building songwriters. Latterly though he was obviously flattered by John Lennon's interest in him at the BMI dinner while the personal visit from the notoriously private Dylan also pleased him even if it must have seemed as surreally unlikely one of Bob's own drug-fuelled 1960s' lyrics. During this period Doc gave also at least one on camera interview – and probably many more because the American music media loved him – in which he maintained, not entirely consistently, that for him song writing was a vocation, something you simply had to do no matter what anyone else thought. This idealistic philosophy did not sit easily with those who remembered Doc's pragmatic entry into song writing being on the grounds that it looked like a more profitable way of making a living than blues shouting. Nor did it chime with his interviews in which he was eager to tell music reporters that he and Mort were simply serving up the songs the kids wanted, songs, he made it clear, that were not to his taste.

In the summer of 1990 Raoul Felder threw a joint birthday party for Doc and himself at Katz's Delicatessen in Manhattan's East Village at a point in the calendar approximately midway between their two birth dates, May 13 and June 27. Jerry Leiber and Mike Stoller attended as did Phil Spector, Lou Reed and Dr. John. Lou Dobbs, the long-serving CNN anchor came and so did Martha Stewart. They say the New York Police Commissioner attended as well although it is not known whether it was for the music or the pastrami or to keep an eye on future convicts Phil Spector and Martha Stewart. It was a memorable night with many more turning up to fête Jerome and Raoul, both of whose careers might be said to have been enhanced – one by accident, one by intention – by Mort Shuman who was not present. Raoul was now one of the city's top divorce lawyers following his sensational debut with Mort's famous divorce settlement, and brother Jerome had taken on the kid Mort most casually to help him expand the appeal of his songs, with, it must be said, not inconsiderable success.

★ ★ ★

In Mort's absence the French, perhaps realising belatedly what they had lost, had issued the album *Mortimer, Ses Plus Belle Chansons*, a greatest hits compilation. In 1990 it went gold and for a few busy weeks Mort diligently undertook a trip to France to promote it through live appearances, TV and radio. The trip took him back to the country he had loved and left but, as ever, for him there was little nostalgia, only a sense of looking forward. "Paris," he once said, "is a very seductive city. You get seduced by the sophistication and the sophistry and all that. You do get hooked in and then you realise it's not what you really want. And then you come back to London."

In 1990 Mort also met Eleanor Bergstein, the woman who had fired innumerable hearts with passion when she wrote *Dirty Dancing*, the memorable 1987 Patrick Swayze/Jennifer Grey film romance. Yet another Jewish Brooklynite, Eleanor told Mort how much she had wanted to use 'Save The Last Dance For Me' in that film, which became a worldwide box office smash with a soundtrack album that sold over 40 million copies. They had never been able to agree publishing terms for the song's inclusion so everyone lost out. Mort was unhappy that he had never known about her request but immediately counted Eleanor Bergstein among his friends.

Back in London he also met at last with Mike Ockrent to try to further his plans for that *Bicycle Thieves* musical, but it would prove another project that was never to be realised.

One project that would be completed – and most satisfyingly – was an album, Mort's last, which would not just signal a move away from his latter day image as a singer of romantic French *chansons*, but stand as a fine piece of work in its own right. During 1990 he recorded its 12 English-language songs with sterling support from a cadre of British musicians that included Rod Argent, Russ Ballard, Peter Van Hooke, Tim Renwick, Clem Clempson and Mo Foster. Mort Shuman wrote or co-wrote all of the songs, one of his various collaborators being Doc Pomus. This last album, titled *Distant Drum*, would feature Mort's version of Pomus/Shuman's final joint composition, 'You Can't Make A Woman Love You'.

11

Last Dances

Mort Shuman was not one for looking back. When something was done it was done and perhaps the closest he ever came to revisiting past glories had been that brief, failed bid to write again with Doc in the late 1980s. When he broke off that short and ultimately unsatisfactory reunion it was not for the old youthful reasons of craving diversions (he had since proved himself more than capable of undertaking almost superhuman workloads), but almost certainly because he knew that you cannot recapture the past. In even his best-natured radio interviews he could not disguise the occasional indifferent tone when responding to the host's well-researched inquiry into some vanished minutiae that Mort had clearly dismissed as unimportant years ago. When Stuart Colman probed to discover just how excited the young Mort must have been when Elvis recorded his melodies he got the breezy response:"Couldn't care less". It hadn't mattered in the 1960s and he wouldn't now pretend that it had done. Despite this tendency he was obliged to revisit the Pomus–Shuman days just once more in the first half of 1991. Doc Pomus, the seemingly indestructible old war horse, had finally succumbed to lung cancer. He had first experienced breathing difficulties in the smoky atmosphere of Katz's at that joint birthday celebration the year before and things were getting worse. Then in January of 1991 Doc's increasing shortness of breath was finally diagnosed by doctors at the NYU Medical Center as being caused by inoperable tumours. He was given a maximum of three months to live. On March 14 he died. He was 65 years old.

It seems uncharitable to assume that Doc's creative life had ended when he split up with Mort Shuman. True, he chose to give up music for years in favour of poker, a game whose adherents may claim it possesses a certain kind of creativity all its own, but Doc saw poker mainly as a potentially entertaining way to make money while pursuing his lifelong passion for drawing colourful characters into his orbit. There is no evidence that he ever won much money and those smoke-filled gambling venues not only alienated Shirlee Hauser but doubtless also contributed to Doc's ill-health.

Gradually he was rediscovered as a treasurable figure from a bright and poppy period of American music that began to enjoy new appreciation, as do many phases that must first pass through a period of unfashionability before being reassessed and revalued. At that point Doc's creativity became that of the guru or professional life coach – albeit a sometimes irascible one. To be sure he had tried writing with various partners on and off, but the unspoken – and perhaps to Doc the unspeakable – truth was that maddening Mortie had been the musical catalyst that somehow brought the best out of Doc's lyrics. It had been Morty's catchy melodies that made many of their songs hits and Doc's lyrics, no matter how good, were simply a plus, not the main reason the records sold. To be fair, sometimes there were other reasons, such as when Elvis Presley recorded their songs guaranteeing automatic success at some level, or when the inspired Leiber and Stoller were producing, especially for The Drifters. Even so, as Doc lay in his last hospital room, the glory days were long gone even if his role as a magnet for friends, family and assorted admirers was undiminished. He loved holding court but knowing he had so little time left meant that these were bitter pleasures.

The Riverside Funeral Home was the setting for Doc's last opportunity to grab the attention of an audience, and this particular gathering included Ahmet Ertegun, Phil Spector, Lou Reed and Mac Rebbenack with many more in attendance and a crowd outside hearing the service relayed on speakers. Jimmy Scott sang 'Someone To Watch Over Me' to what was probably his biggest ever audience. They say that on the way out of the chapel Seymour Stein of Sire Records demonstrated that exquisitely maladroit sense of timing for which the record business was so justly famous and buttonholed Scott with a view to offering him a record deal on the strength of his performance that day. The man Doc had tirelessly promoted for years with virtually no success would finally get his break after unwittingly giving an audition at his chief supporter's wake. As Doc might have said, "D'ya believe this shit?"

They buried him on Long Island in the Beth David Cemetery at Elmont, Nassau County. Millie and Morris lay interred nearby and one wonders whether anyone had the nerve to suggest that their tombstones should be inscribed, 'Reconciled At Last'. Doc's stone is positively wordy, as perhaps befits a lyric writer, and after death he still seems to be giving advice:

Doc Pomus
Jerome Solon Felder
June 27, 1925 – March 14, 1991
Turning Corners Is Only A State Of Mind
Keeping Your Eyes Closed Is Worse Than Being Blind
There Is Always One More Time – DP
Save The Last Dance For Me

★ ★ ★

In Britain Mort wrote a characteristically humane and irreverent obituary of Doc Pomus for the magazine *Now Dig This!* in which he characterised his subject as "… mentor, professor, big brother, sometime father figure, asshole buddy, and partner all at the same time". He described their mutual good fortune when they first met at a time when Doc's blues gigs were getting thin on the ground as "a crossroads in (Doc's) life … I just fell in kind of like a signpost pointing to rock'n'roll heaven."

As for Doc's physical handicap Mort note, "Lots of people bent over backwards to make his life in motion easier. I don't think they did him any great favours. Some of us just told him to move his ass when we knew he could do it."

He also made an oblique and unspecific dig at some of the women in Doc's life whose dutiful attentions Mort seemed to feel sometimes looked like doing penance. Penance for what? He does not say, but one suspects he may have been wondering if Doc's fondness for young, blonde girls with little experience of life seemed doomed to draw them into intimacy before they knew what they wanted so that when they grew up and left him, they overcompensated. His final nod to "the greatest blue-eyed blues shouter of them all" was to "say goodbye to my partner who taught me so much. Mostly about myself."

Doc Pomus' reputation gradually grew in the years following his death. His daughter Sharyn and her husband Will Bratton (who runs Pomus Songs Inc.) have devoted much energy to elevating his reputation – sometimes, even the most neutral observer might think – with the secondary ambition of airbrushing Mort Shuman out of the picture.

★ ★ ★

By 1991 Mort too was visibly in poor health. He suffered two minor strokes and was diagnosed with liver cancer. No longer able to drink alcohol and looking older and more drawn, he nonetheless remained active, writing and producing the music for a French TV series called *Salut Les Copains*, a durable catch-all retro title in French popular culture (meaning something like 'Hi There Buddies') that half a century ago adorned a teen magazine, became the name of a 1961 Johnny Hallyday album and in 2012 would be the title of a French musical comedy focussing on the *yé yé* days of the 1960s and 1970s. The *Salut Les Copains* TV series for which Mort wrote the music would first air in November of 1991 and spawned an accompanying album with performances by Mort, his old friend Eddy Mitchell and Florence Caillon.

Mort's *Distant Drum* album was released by EastWest Records/ Atlantic, notionally reuniting him with the old label where he had sung and sold publishing rights to 'The Curtain Fell' over 30 years before, the label for which all those classic Drifters songs had been recorded. A single was released and, against the odds, Mort again undertook a series of promotional activities for TV, radio and press, this time mostly in Germany where the album had its first release. The planned full programme of promotions was cut short by Mort's further deteriorating health and this resulted in a muffled UK release for what was an extraordinarily good album that seemed to explore many of Mort Shuman's preoccupations in quite new and fresh ways.

The first track, 'Promised Land', was a natural choice for a single. With its punchy and catchy horn riffs it nodded in the direction of the classic Atlantic years while its refrain 'I'm a stranger in a promised land' suggested an element of vulnerability that was echoed in Mort's voice which at the same time manages to sound as natural, assured and as musical as ever. This final selection of performances of Mort on disc is a reminder that as a singer he was protean. When he was Pomus and Shuman's demo maker back in the 1960s his job was only to illustrate this or that song for prospective artists to whom the sheet music would have meant nothing. Even so he would occasionally sound as if he was giving an audition, anxious to demonstrate that despite the limitations of the local studio he could sing the hell out of a ballad, a light pop song, or a driving rock number, as the material demanded. His demo for 'Wide Wide World' is quite simply superior to Del Shannon's final version and we should recall that even Elvis thought that some of Mort's musical touches were worth copying on record.

'Sorrow' revisits one of his greatest French hits, a song that was originally featured in *A Nous Les Petites Anglaises!* 'Just Before The Fall' is a fine example of Mort's mature song writing and proof that as well as his dazzling musicianship he had become a fine lyricist capable of melding the rhythmic demands of melody and words into a single satisfying whole.

'Amalie' is a superb and atmospheric song afloat on the imagery of tropical storms, sexual longing and impending doom, with more than a faint whiff of rum about it. 'You Can't Make A Woman Love You' is a Pomus/Shuman song once recorded by disco pioneer George McCrae, and it sounds like Mort's farewell nod to Doc even though this album was completed before Doc's death. 'Closer' celebrates his writing partnership with Eric Blau. The album's haunting final track, 'Just An Hour', bids fair to outdo 'Doin' The Best I Can' in the rejected love stakes. Its narrative of a young man committing the cardinal sin of falling in love with a prostitute is shot through with the painful realisation that he will never be able to afford more than an hour of her time when of course the only thing that will ever satisfy him is to take her away forever.

Who can say what would have happened to *Distant Drum* had the old indefatigable Mort been well enough to promote it? Thunderbird Records reissued it in 1999 and it remains one of the most intimate and richly-textured albums he ever recorded. Musical taste is a highly personal and therefore unpredictable thing, but whether the record buying public would have made it a hit or let it slip by as a worthy niche album, one thing is certain: Mort Shuman was still looking to the future even when he knew his own future was about to be cut short.

★ ★ ★

In a pleasingly symmetrical coincidence Doc Pomus in his final days had also been working towards an album that he felt might be some sort of summation of his writing even though he had no plans to record it himself. His collaboration with Mac Rebbenack had produced a clutch of blues songs, these still being the only kind of songs Doc really wanted to write. With the exception of one track, 'Still In Love', Doc's contribution, as ever lay mainly, in supplying lyrics while Rebbenack wrote the music to all but three of the other songs on the 12-track album. Joe Kookoolis, Ken Hirsch and Mort Shuman were the other three co-writers. 'No One' was the Pomus/ Shuman number, once recorded by Ray Charles, Connie Francis and Brenda Lee but here to be sung, like all the other tracks, by Johnny Adams on an album called *The Real Me* released on the Rounder label in late 1991. Johnny Adams (Laten John Adams) had been one of Doc's favourite blues singers, perhaps because his dazzling array of vocal tricks brought something fresh to the intrinsically limited framework of the blues song. Adams' most successful record dated from 1969 when he had a hit with 'Reconsider Me', a country/ soul ballad written by Margaret Lewis and Mira Smith, given in a virile vocal performance interlaced with sensational falsetto swoops. Adams had been produced on and off by Mac Rebbenack since both of them were teenagers so he was a natural choice for *The Real Me* which was subtitled *Johnny Adams Sings Doc Pomus*. Rebbenack co-produced with Scott Billington and although the album found favour with some critics it also reinforced what Doc had never tried to disguise: that, yes, he was just an old blues writer, albeit a good one. *The Real Me* dressed up its songs to make them sound more interesting, except in the case of 'No One' which Adams managed to make less interesting by giving it the kind of jazz -lite treatment that MOR entertainers used to apply to pop songs they felt were beneath them and therefore in need of a layer of what they imagined to be sophistication.

★ ★ ★

Ray Connolly remembers phoning Mort hoping to catch up with him in the autumn of 1991. Mort told him that he had just had a liver transplant. "Soon afterwards I read in *The Times* that he had died."

★　★　★

The funeral of Mortimer Shuman, born in Brooklyn, musician extraordinaire, gastronome, wine connoisseur, enthusiastic globetrotter, Anglophile and honorary Frenchman, was held at The Hoop Lane Jewish Cemetery in Golders Green, northwest London. He had died on November 2, 1991, ten days short of his 55th birthday, after a brave but hopeless battle against liver cancer ending in a failed transplant. Not all of the old gang from his Parisian days were still around but, in addition to a clutch of British friends and colleagues that included Don Black and other members of the archly named SODS (Society Of Distinguished Songwriters), a surprising number of French friends and colleagues made the short-notice trip across the channel to pay their respects and comfort Maria-Pia and their daughters. It was a remarkable turnout in the light of the logistical demands imposed by Jewish funerals that take place the day after death. Singers Johnny Hallyday, Eddy Mitchell and Philippe Lavil as well as long-time artistic director of the French radio station RTL Monique LeMarcis were there. Mort's faithful press agent Tony Krantz came with a heart-shaped wreath of roses. Also present were Nicole Savourat from Phonogram, TV producer Leila Milcic and Mort's old Parisian carousing buddy Gérard Baqué.

After the ceremony Johnny Hallyday asked Gérard Baqué to call him if Maria-Pia needed anything, and then returned to France where he cut Mort's song 'Dans Un An Ou Un Jour' ('In A Year Or A Day'), making sure that the words 'À mon ami Mort Shuman' appeared after the title.

Back in central London Baqué and a British member of the old Parisian gang Richard White repaired to a hotel bar where, confident that it was what the departed would have wanted, downed Bull Shots in memory of their old pal.

Some years later Mort's remains were transferred to Caudéran to the west of Bordeaux – Maria-Pia's home town – and his grave is now to be found at the Cimitière des Pins-Francs, Bordeaux- Caudéran, a regional cemetery where first-time visitors are sometimes surprised to discover that this is the final resting place of Mortimer Shuman, erstwhile songwriter to The King and, in his day, a French superstar.

12

Coda

Doc Pomus had lent his name to an Artist Assistance Fund which was the first grant programme to be launched by the not-for-profit Rhythm and Blues Foundation and was intended to address the immediate needs of distressed performers. The Foundation had been established in the wake of a dispute between Ruth Brown (Ruth Alston Weston) 'The Queen Of R&B' and Ahmet Ertegun over the poor financial returns she had received for her many successful Atlantic recordings. The Rhythm and Blues Foundation made Doc an honoree in its 1990/91 inductions. He was the first white recipient of that distinction.

In 1992 Phil Spector inducted Doc into The Rock and Roll Hall Of Fame, an honour that was perhaps wisely conferred post mortem since, whisper it gently, Doc didn't care for rock'n'roll all that much.

Sharyn Felder helped steer into being an excellent 1995 Rhino album *Till The Night Is Gone* featuring new and sometimes imaginative versions of some familiar songs performed by Bob Dylan, Shawn Colvin, Lou Reed, Rosanne Cash, Los Lobos and others. Only its subtitle, *A Tribute To Doc Pomus,* betrays its role in the agenda to reinvent Doc as dominant author of the Pomus-Shuman oeuvre. The majority of the songs on it were composed by Mort Shuman, with words by Doc Pomus. Shawn Colvin's chilling reading of 'Viva Las Vegas' did not please all critics but for some of us it managed to pull off two quite unexpectedly brilliant tricks: firstly it illuminates the polar difference between winning and losing in Sin City by turning a brash song of fluorescent celebration into a hauntingly ironic lament; secondly it shows that a Pomus-Shuman number many originally dismissed as a routine title theme for an Elvis movie is actually a very good song if you look (or rather listen) beyond the glitz.

In 2012 Sharyn Felder's documentary about her father, *A.K.A. Doc Pomus*, started doing the rounds of the US film festivals. Judging by the trailer it looks like a rather partisan project that already seems to be enjoying some success at persuading others to toe the party line. One unidentified commentator who looks very much like Ken Emerson, author of a good book about the Brill Building era *Always Magic In The Air*, can be seen intoning that out of the pain of his polio-stricken youth Doc Pomus "was able to produce some of the most romantic, yearning, innocent music that is about as deep and as truthful and as beautiful as popular music can be". Music? Doc wrote the words. After this inaccurate accolade the trailer cuts to Andy Williams singing the Pomus-Shuman song that he loathed, 'Can't Get Used To Losing You'.

Even Doc's friend Peter Guralnick, author of many well-respected rock books, appears to be infected by the hagiographic spirit of Sharyn Felder when he writes in his liner notes for Johnny Adams' *The Real Me*: "In another culture Doc Pomus might have been considered a legitimate composer, and in fact his model as a young writer was Irving Berlin". In another culture perhaps, but in the culture he inhabited Doc Pomus was not really a composer at all, he was a lyricist. Irving Berlin was, supremely, both.

★ ★ ★

Soon after Mort's death two events were held to celebrate his life. One in London was presented by his British manager Charles Negus-

Fancey and Don Black with contributions from Tim Rice, Errol Brown and Sandie Shaw and eulogies from Ahmet Ertegun, Dion Di Mucci, Freddie Bienstock and Eleanor Bergstein. Another, held in New York, had contributions from Eric Blau, Harriet Holtsman, Aaron Schechter, Joe Neal, Paul Felder, Sean Elliot and Elly Stone.

Jacques Brel Is Alive And Well And Living In Paris had two successful Los Angeles revivals in quick succession: in 2010 at The Colony Theatre and in 2011 at The Met Theatre.

Mort Shuman was also inducted into The Rock and Roll Hall Of Fame although not until 2010 which is strange since it must surely have been in recognition of his rock'n' oll songs written with Doc Pomus who had been inducted 18 years earlier. By 2010 Phil Spector was in no position to do the honours having himself been inducted into the California Substance Abuse Treatment Facility and State Prison in Corcoran, California. Mort was made the recipient of the Ahmet Ertegun Award along with David Geffen, Barry Mann & Cynthia Weil, Jeff Barry, Ellie Greenwich, Otis Blackwell and Jesse Stone. The ceremony took place at The Waldorf Astoria in New York where Maria-Pia Shuman accepted Mort's award in the company of Steve Van Zandt, Cynthia Weil, Barry Mann and Otis Blackwell Jnr.

★   ★   ★

Now that they have gone, Doc and Mort's lives and careers become gradually reshaped by the cumulative recollections of those who knew them. Doc was in every sense a larger-than-life character who in the memory of many of his friends excelled as an astringent commentator on countless scams and fraudulent music business shenanigans, not because he himself perpetrated them but because he simply loved outrageous chicanery, telling and retelling scabrous industry anecdotes to his shifting retinue over the years. Often short-changed and swindled by the proprietors of all those clubs and dives he worked in his early days, Doc had a store of such stories the telling of which placed him squarely shoulder to shoulder with all those musicians who had ever been exploited over the years. He liked to tell of how he had once asked George Goldner, the owner of Roulette Records, what he would do if a record company was swindling him out of royalties. Goldner replied, "I'd sue them." "OK," said, Doc, "I'm going to sue you."

Doc always had to have an enemy, and in later years it was a role usually played by the villain of one of his anecdotes, some shyster who didn't pay, skipped town or double-crossed. Capable of being both cynical and sentimental Doc was essentially a generous and intelligent man whom fate had dealt the cruellest of blows when he was a child. When he dragged himself up on that stage at George's Tavern it was an act of almost unimaginable heroism that would have been beyond many of us for whom, in his circumstances, simple survival might have been enough. Doc's refusal to be 'a happy cripple', to use his much-quoted phrase, meant that he demanded more. To paraphrase William Faulkner, he wanted not just to survive but to subdue and to flourish. He did not want to be defined by his disability, but of course he was, even when he was being admired for his courage. It got in the way, whatever he did.

Mort Shuman was incomparably luckier than Doc but it was not luck that brought about a dazzling career in music which, had it all played out in the US, would have made him a huge star there and as a consequence in many other places as well. As things turned out his French successes effectively isolated him from both the US and the UK for many years. Where luck and temperament did favour him was in having a personality so warm that it is difficult to find anyone who knew him who was not overwhelmed with his generosity of spirit and boundless appetite for life – perhaps 'lust for life' would be a better choice of phrase for *bon viveur* and ladies' man Mort if only it did not evoke for moviegoers of a certain age the image of Kirk Douglas impersonating Van Gogh with a bandage around his head. No one who knew Mort seems to need any encouragement to start talking adoringly about him – indeed they usually need help in stopping. This benign image of course ignores his somewhat cavalier treatment of his widowed mother when he was young and takes no account of the peremptorily dumped girlfriends of his Lothario years and a worryingly glib passing reference to abortions in his notes for a biography. If he was not, as he himself admitted, a driven man, there is still the occasional glint of steel visible beneath the surface of his defections, not just from Doc but from other partners, personal and professional, whom he left as soon as he was ready even if they weren't. But in the end his force of personality, his warmth and his prodigious musical gifts prevailed and these are what animate most people's personal memories of him. So what if his contributions to the Pomus-Shuman hit-making partnership have sometimes been unfairly played down in order to aggrandize Doc's reputation?

Believing this to be the case was one of the original reasons for my writing this book; it was an attempt to rebalance the books. Now having explored Mort Shuman's rich, productive and sometimes maddeningly elusive life, the scale of his achievement seems to be almost embarrassingly self-evident. It is more or less beyond argument that the pop melodies Mort wrote with Doc were more than 50% responsible for their success. Mort Shuman's sustained achievements as a composer in France where he worked with a succession of lyricists for over a dozen years – Étienne Roda-Gil, Philippe Adler, Patrick Ageron, Claude LeMesle, Renée Benveniste, Élisabeth Moreau, Pierre Delanoë, Christian Éclimont, Michel Mallory and several more – clearly show that it was his music that consistently created hits, not any individual lyricist's words, important as they might be. In Britain, Kenny Lynch wrote rather good lyrics but he never had memorable hits like 'Love's Just A Broken Heart' and 'Sha La La La Lee' until he wrote with Mort. Don Black, a contemporary lyricist of high international repute, a collaborator with John Barry, Andrew Lloyd Webber, Jule Styne and Quincy Jones, judged Mort to be a very fine composer, particularly well-attuned to writing for musical theatre.

In contrast Doc Pomus, who admired Irving Berlin, actually hated musicals even though he once agreed to write songs for a Broadway show about Elvis with Bruce Foster. The show went from Broadway directly to Las Vegas and Doc's verdict was, "I was so embarrassed about being connected with it". Doc continued to resent any suggestions that he should write songs for the musical theatre, once saying, "My kids said it was our music that was going to stay around. I wrote it the same way I would write a symphony but I have no reason for thinking it would last. I don't think that Leiber and Stoller got it in perspective, they got scarred by the old-time songwriters and they wanted to do Broadway shows." Again one wonders how even the most accomplished lyricist could have imagined approaching pop and blues song writing as if it were a symphony, a form which has no words. Where is the evidence – apart from the pleasant 'Heartlessly', the derivative 'Lonely Avenue', the routine 'Boogie Woogie Country Girl' and a clutch of frankly repetitive and primitive blues shouting songs – that Doc wrote much music at all? During the Pomus-Shuman heyday he did no more than make the occasional musical suggestion to Mort Shuman just as, *quid pro quo*, Mort Shuman might make the occasional suggestion to him about the lyrics.

Whatever the vagaries of posterity's opinion, Pomus & Shuman's joint legacy is now part of popular music history, having seeped into the folk memory in a way that, strangely enough, the often brilliant songs of Leiber and Stoller have not always managed to do. Perhaps in part it has something to do with how often Leiber and Stoller concentrated on writing witty songs aimed at The Coasters, songs which were rooted in the mundane experiences of young urban black kids – 'Charlie Brown' the class clown; 'Yakety Yak' and its comic theme of parental nagging; and 'Shopping For Clothes', a sublime vignette of the young hipster in a clothes store carefully assembling his ideal wardrobe before his failed credit check puts an end to his shopping spree. They were great songs but they were too much of their time and place to be classics. Of course Leiber and Stoller wrote some excellent songs for Elvis too as well as for many other artists and their partnership is assured of a high place in pop history. What is more, excluding the triumphant multi-hit Pomus & Shuman year of 1961, overall Leiber and Stoller almost certainly outstripped even Doc and Mort's 30 million+ total sales. Yet the keening sound of 'Teenager In Love', the driving blues-rock complaint of 'Little Sister', the infectious joy of 'This Magic Moment', the sheer emotion of 'Save The Last Dance For Me' and the dramatic angst of 'Suspicion' all seem to have a kind of universality of appeal that enables them to travel very well down the years. In 2012 and 2013 a UK touring production of a new musical called 'Save The Last Dance For Me' demonstrated how effortlessly Pomus-Shuman songs can illuminate a love story far removed from the time and place in which they were originally written. With a book by Laurence Marks and Maurice Gran, creators of several successful British TV sitcoms, the new context for these songs owes nothing to Ray Connolly's scenario of New Yorkers under threat of possible nuclear war and is set instead in a drab English seaside town in 1963 where two young sisters on holiday encounter an American airman who invites them to a dance at the nearby United States Air Force base. As much about the allure of American popular music for pre-Beatles British youth as it is about its central love story, the show rather cleverly makes the songs an intrinsic part of the heady atmosphere of romance, not just artfully inserted commentaries upon it.

In 2004 *Dirty Dancing* writer Eleanor Bergstein adapted her film script for the stage and the production opened in Sydney, Australia in November of that year with new productions to follow in London's West End as well as in Europe and North America. Thirteen years after the deaths of Doc and Mort she had finally secured permission to include 'Save The Last Dance For Me' and 'This Magic Moment' as well as 'Teenager In Love' for some productions.

Little musical gems that caught the Zeitgeist of the late 1950s and early 1960s, those songs and a dozen or so more by Pomus-Shuman have lasted half a century and now look destined to endure indefinitely. The brief span of years when they were written marked the twilight of Doc Pomus' career and the dawn of Mort Shuman's extraordinary musical adventures across two continents. When they were together no one – certainly not Pomus and Shuman themselves – ever believed that they were doing much more than making a buck while writing disposable pop music to match the mood of the passing moment... and certainly they wrote very many songs that missed the mark and sank without trace. Doc certainly had "no reason for thinking it would last". And at moments when things looked to be in danger of being taken too seriously, Mort was fond of saying in an exaggerated Brooklyn accent "We ain't making noive gas here".

There was no pretence that they were creating art. Still, just as pretension cannot make art out of dross, neither can lack of pretension prevent art from coming about anyway if the work is good enough. Often enough, in Pomus and Shuman's heyday, it was. What happened before and after that pivotal period was a story of two songwriters who were, together and apart, unlike any other in the annals of popular music.

Sources & Thanks

Aknin, Alain-Guy, & Loisy, Stéphane Loisy. *Mort Shuman, Le Géant de Porcelaine* (Éditions Didier Carpentier)

Clayson, Alan & Leigh, Spencer (eds). *Aspects Of Elvis, Tryin' To Get To You* (ISBN 0-283-06217-7

Emerson, Ken. *Always Magic In The Air* (ISBN 0-670-03456-8, Viking)

Friedman, Jay Alan. *Tell The Truth Until They Bleed: Coming Clean In The Dirty World Of Blues And Rock 'N' Roll* (ISBN: 0-879-30932-6, Backbeat Books)

Goldberger, Alex. *The City Observed* (ISBN 0-140-46496-6, Penguin

Guralnick, Peter. Sleeve notes to Johnny Adams' *The Real Me* album

Halberstadt, Alex. *Lonely Avenue* (ISBN 978-0-306-81564-5, Da Capo Press

Leigh, Spencer. 'My Room Has Got Two Windows' (four-part feature that ran in the magazine *Now Dig This* from June to September, 2003

Mailer, Norman. *The White Negro* (1957, City Lights)

Palmer Rober. Booklet text for *The Birth Of Soul* boxed set of Ray Charles' Complete Atlantic Rhythm & Blues Recordings, 1952-1959

Pouzenc, Jean-Marie. Booklet text for *Elvis Chante Mort Shuman & Doc Pomus*

Rogan Johnny. *The Complete Guide To The Music of The Smiths* (1995, Omnibus Press)

Sidgwick & Jackson)

Stewart, Douglas T, with Blake, Norman. 'The Life & Death Of Mort' (2009 retrospective liner notes for the Rev-Ola re-issue of the Reprise album *My Death* by Mort Shuman)

Whitcomb, Ian. *Whole Lotta Shakin'* (ISBN 0-099-27170-2, Arrow Books)

Willensky, Elliot. *When Brooklyn Was The World* (ISBN 0-517-55858-0, Harmony Books, New York)

mortshuman.com is a rich source of information about Mort Shuman that includes several of his demo tracks, many audio clips including interviews, the full text of his brief notes for an autobiography and many recollections from friends and colleagues.

★   ★   ★

Particular thanks are due to Charles Negus-Fancey, Maria-Pia Shuman, Don Black and Ray Connolly. Spencer Leigh's comprehensive published writings about Doc Pomus and Mort Shuman provided a level of background information and discographical detail that would take a lifetime to replicate. Spencer's happily preserved audio interviews with Mort Shuman, like those of Stuart Colman, offered informal and sometimes very revealing insights unavailable elsewhere.

Index

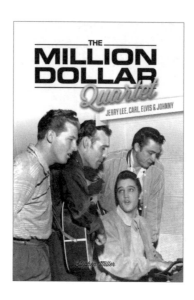

THE MILLION DOLLAR QUARTET

By Stephen Miller

The near-mythic day of The Million Dollar Quartet is here explored in minute detail in a fascinating book that features new interviews and key reminiscences of some of those involved.

The spontaneous get-together of Elvis Presley, Carl Perkins, Johnny Cash and Jerry Lee Lewis at Sun Records in Memphis took place on December 4, 1956. Elvis was the only bona fide superstar having already left the label and its owner Sam Phillips for RCA Records and Hollywood. Perkins was trying to capitalise on his hit 'Blue Suede Shoes' while Cash and Lewis were yet to attain major fame and notoriety.

Presley dropped in during a Perkins session featuring Lewis on piano, and, with the exception of Cash who joined them but did not sing, they started performing the kind of songs they loved – three young guys making music for themselves. Phillips recorded the spontaneous session and eventually the tape would surface in the 1970s to become the subject of many a legal wrangle before achieving an official release. As a result we can now hear the music, but this book is surely as close as anyone will ever come to being a fly on the wall of Sun Studios during that historic jam session over half a century ago.

Available from **www.omnibuspress.com**

ISBN: 978.1.78038.514.3
Order No: OP54692

ALL HOPPED UP AND READY TO GO
Music From The Street Of New York 1927-77
By Tony Fletcher

From the acclaimed biographer of Keith Moon comes an incisive history of New York's seminal music scenes, encompassing the ways in which the city's indigenous art, literature, theatre and political movements converged to create such unique sounds, as well as the music's vast contributions to our culture.

With great attention to the characters, from trumpet player Dizzy Gillespie to Tito Puente, Bob Dylan to the Ramones, *All Hopped Up And Ready To Go* takes us through bebop, the Latin music scene, the folk revival, glitter music, disco, punk and hip-hop, as they emerged from the neighbourhood streets of Harlem, the Village, Brooklyn, Bronx and Queens.

Fletcher's narrative hurtles along like a high-speed cab ride down Broadway. – MOJO magazine

... covers a dazzling array of eras and genres – and expertly traces the lines between them. – Q magazine

I enjoyed this book almost as much as I originally enjoyed all the music it covered. – Peter Buck, R.E.M.

Available from **www.omnibuspress.com**

ISBN: 978.1.84938.244.1
Order No: OP53273

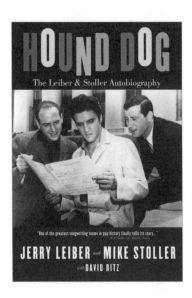

HOUND DOG
The Leiber & Stoller Autobiography
By Jerry Leiber & Mike Stoller

With David Ritz

The fascinating and irreverent story of rock'n'roll's number one songwriting partnership!

When Jerry Leiber and Mike Stoller first met in 1950 it marked the beginning of a legendary collaboration that parlayed the spirit of American R&B into a string of international rock'n'roll hits. Elvis Presley, The Coasters, Ben E. King, The Drifters and Peggy Lee were just some of the acts who enjoyed huge successes with their songs. 'Hound Dog', 'Jailhouse Rock', 'I'm A Woman' and 'Yakety Yak' were among the most famous numbers in a stellar Leiber & Stoller catalogue that eventually inspired long-running jukebox musical *Smokey Joe's Café*.

Leiber & Stoller were inducted into the Songwriters Hall Of Fame in 1985 and The Rock & Roll Hall Of Fame in 1987. Their extraordinary story is an inextricable part of the history of American popular music from the 1950s onwards.

David Ritz has collaborated on books with Ray Charles, Aretha Franklin, Marvin Gaye and Smokey Robinson, among others. He is also co-writer of the song 'Sexual Healing' with Marvin Gaye and Odell Brown.

Available from **www.omnibuspress.com**

ISBN: 978.1.84938.249.4
Order No: OP53658

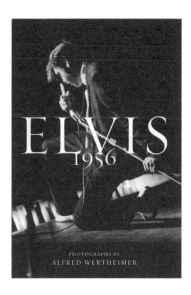

ELVIS 1956
Photographs by Alfred Wertheimer

Taken during the year Elvis turned 21, Alfred Wertheimer's legendary photographs are a remarkable visual record of a defining time for rock'n'roll's most enduring figure.

The year is 1956. When Elvis walked on stage time stopped – and then exploded. The earth shook on its axis and the beat of everyday life was jolted. In an instant, mainstream America's veneer of cultural complacency evaporated.

Elvis Presley was about to become the greatest rocker in the history of rock'n'roll. Here is Elvis before he became the prisoner of his own celebrity. Soon his manager, Colonel Tom Parker, would put an end to all unmanaged reporting. Never again would anyone capture the essential freshness and vigour of these impromptu photographs. Never again would anyone be allowed to see the man behind the myth. Elvis 1956 shows us the King before the curtain fell – Elvis at his most innocent, most vulnerable, most intensely charismatic – Elvis in the last moments before the man became a legend.

Available from **www.omnibuspress.com**

ISBN: 978.1.78305.048.2
Order No: OP55385